THE ONE YEAR BOOK OF
Personal Prayer

THE
ONE
YEAR®
BOOK OF
Personal
Prayer

Inspirational Prayers and Thoughts
for Each Day of the Year

Tyndale House Publishers, Inc.
WHEATON, ILLINOIS

The prayers and quotes in *The One Year Book of Personal Prayer* were collected and edited by Daniel Partner. The idea for this book originated with, and was introduced by, Bruce Barton. Mark R. Norton served as the Tyndale House coordinating and advisory editor, and Julee Schwarzburg served as the production coordinator. The interior and cover of this book were designed by Timothy R. Botts.

Copyright © 1991 by Tyndale House Publishers, Inc., Wheaton, Illinois.

The *"NIV"* and *"New International Version"* trademarks are registered in the United States Patent and Trademark Office by International Bible Society. All rights reserved.

The One Year is a registered trademark of Tyndale House Publishers, Inc.

All Scripture quotations, unless otherwise noted, are from *The Holy Bible, New International Version®*. Copyright © 1973, 1978, 1984 by International Bible Society. Used by permission of Zondervan Publishing House. All rights reserved.

Scripture quotations marked TLB are from *The Living Bible*. Copyright © 1971 owned by assignment by KNT Charitable Trust. All rights reserved.

Scripture quotations marked NKJV are from *The Holy Bible,* New King James Version. Copyright © 1979, 1980, 1982, Thomas Nelson Inc., Publishers.

Scripture quotations marked NRSV are from *The Holy Bible,* the New Revised Standard Version. Copyright © 1989 by the Division of Christian Education of the National Council of the Churches of Christ in the United States of America, and are used by permission. All rights reserved.

Scripture quotations marked KJV are from *The Holy Bible,* Authorized King James Version.

Front cover photo copyright © 1992 Gary Irving.

Library of Congress Catalog Card Number 91-65120
Softcover ISBN 0-8423-2616-2
Hardcover ISBN 0-8423-2698-7
Printed in the United States of America

97 96 95 94 93
10 9   8   7   6   5

Copyright Acknowledgments

One of the prayers of Anselm of Canterbury (Mar. 24) is from *The Prayers and Meditations of St. Anselm*, translated by Sister Benedicta Ward, S L G (Penguin Classics, 1973), copyright © 1973 by Benedicta Ward.

The prayers of George Appleton (Mar. 15, 21) are reprinted from *The Oxford Book of Prayer*, edited by George Appleton (1985), by permission of Oxford University Press on behalf of the author.

The prayers of John Baillie (Jan. 10; Mar. 3; Apr. 30; May 13; June 13; July 8, 15; Aug. 23; Sept. 5; Oct. 18; Nov. 3) are reprinted with permission of Charles Scribner's Sons, an imprint of MacMillan Publishing Company, and Oxford University Press from *A Diary of Private Prayer*, by John Baillie. Copyright © 1949 Charles Scribner's Sons; copyright renewed © 1977 Ian Fowler Baillie.

The prayers of Dietrich Bonhoeffer (Mar. 26; Apr. 10; Oct. 17) are reprinted with permission of MacMillan Publishing Company and SCM Press, Ltd. from *Letters and Papers from Prison*, by Dietrich Bonhoeffer. Copyright © 1953, 1967, 1971 by SCM Press, Ltd.

The prayers of Avery Brooke (July 30; Aug. 19; Oct. 14; Nov. 5; Dec. 11) are from *Plain Prayers for a Complicated World*, published by Vineyard Books, Inc., 129 Nearwater Lane, Noroton, CT 06820. Copyright © 1975 by Avery Brooke. Used by permission of Vineyard Books, Inc.

The prayers of Ruth Harms Calkin are from *Lord You Love to Say Yes* (Feb. 26; Aug. 6), published by Tyndale House Publishers, Inc., copyright © 1976 by Ruth Harms Calkin; and

Marriage Is So Much More, Lord (Mar. 18) published by Tyndale House Publishers, Inc., copyright © 1979 by Ruth Harms Calkin; and *Lord I Keep Running Back to You* (Apr. 15; May 5; June 19; July 26; Sept. 7) published by Tyndale House Publishers, Inc., copyright © 1979 by Ruth Harms Calkin. Used by permission of Tyndale House Publishers, Inc.

The prayers of John B. Coburn (Sept. 28; Oct. 11; Dec. 12) are from *A Diary of Prayer: Personal and Public*, by John B. Coburn. Copyright © 1975 The Westminster Press. Used by permission of Westminster/John Knox Press.

The prayer of David M. Currie (Feb. 23) is from: *Come, Let Us Worship God: A Handbook of Prayer for Leaders of Worship*, by David M. Currie. Copyright © 1977 The Westminster Press. Used by permission of Westminster/John Knox Press.

The prayers of Ralph S. Cushman (Aug. 5; Sept. 4; Oct. 1; Nov. 11) are from *Hilltop Verses and Prayers*, published by Abingdon Press, copyright © 1945 by Ralph S. Cushman. Reprinted by permission of Robert E. Cushman.

The prayers of Dag Hammarskjöld (Feb. 16; Mar. 31) are from *Markings*, by Dag Hammarskjöld, translated by Leif Sjoberg and W. H. Auden. Translation copyright © 1964 by Alfred A. Knopf, Inc. and Faber & Faber Ltd. Reprinted by permission of Alfred A. Knopf, Inc. and Faber & Faber Ltd.

The prayer of Jack W. Hayford (Apr. 28) is from *Prayer Is Invading the Impossible*, copyright © 1977 by Logos International, Plainfield, New Jersey. Reprinted by permission of Logos International.

The prayers of Michael Hollings and Etta Gullick (Aug. 3; Sept. 3; Oct. 2; Nov. 10; Dec. 20) are from *It's Me, O Lord!* copyright © 1973 by Michael Hollings and Etta Gullick. Used by permission of Doubleday, a division of Bantam Doubleday Dell Publishing Group, Inc., and McCrimmon

Publishing Co. Ltd., Great Wakening, Essex, England. All rights reserved.

The prayer of Sören Kierkegaard (Mar. 26) is from *The Prayers of Kierkegaard,* edited by Perry F. LeFevre, copyright © 1978 by the University of Chicago Press. Used by permission.

The prayers of Martin Luther (Feb. 28, Apr. 6) are from *Devotions and Prayers of Martin Luther,* translated by Andrew Kosten, copyright © Baker Book House, 1956. Used by permission of Baker Book House.

The prayer of Paul Simpson McElroy (Feb. 4) is from *Table Graces, Prayers of Thanks,* copyright © 1986 by Peter Pauper Press, White Plains, New York. Used by permission.

The prayer of Catherine Marshall (May 28) is from *Adventures in Prayer,* by Catherine Marshall. Copyright © 1975 by Catherine Marshall LeSourd. Published by Chosen Books, Flemming H. Revell Company. Used by permission.

The prayers of Peter Marshall (Jan. 29, Apr. 1, May 9) are from *Mr. Jones, Meet the Master,* edited by Catherine Marshall. Copyright © 1949, 1950 by Fleming H. Revell Company. Renewed © 1976, 1977 by Catherine Marshall LeSourd. Used by permission of Chosen Books, Fleming H. Revell Company.

The prayers of Peter Marshall (Feb. 5; June 18; July 16; Aug. 14; Sept. 20; Dec. 25) are from *The Prayers of Peter Marshall,* compiled and edited by Catherine Marshall. Copyright © 1979 by Catherine Marshall LeSourd. Published by Chosen Books, Fleming H. Revell Company. Used by permission.

The prayer of Peter Marshall (Mar. 1) is from *The Best of Peter Marshall,* compiled and edited by Catherine Marshall. Copyright © 1983 by Catherine Marshall LeSourd. Used by permission of Chosen Books, Fleming H. Revell Company.

The prayers identified *My Prayer Book* (Apr. 18; May 14; June 1; July 17; Aug. 10; Sept. 6; Nov. 1) are from *My Prayer Book,* copyright © 1957 by Concordia Publishing House. Reprinted by permission from CPH.

The prayers of Reinhold Niebuhr (Feb. 2, Aug. 11) are from *Justice and Mercy,* by Reinhold Niebuhr, edited by Ursula M. Niebuhr. Copyright © 1974 by Ursula M. Niebuhr. Used by permission of Westminster/John Knox Press.

The prayers of Louis Gifford Parkhurst, Jr. (Feb. 11, Sept. 8) are from *How to Pray in the Spirit,* by John Bunyan, copyright © 1991 by Louis Gifford Parkhurst, Jr. Used by permission of Word (U.K.) Ltd., 9 Holdom Avenue, Bletchly, Milton Keynes, MK1 1QR, England.

The prayers of Daniel Partner (Jan. 12, Feb. 12, Mar. 25, Apr. 21, May 25, June 16, July 6, Aug. 8, Nov. 13, Dec. 21), copyright © 1991 by L. Daniel Partner, were written expressly for *The One Year Book of Personal Prayer.*

The prayer of Alan Paton (Jan. 11) is from *Instrument of Thy Peace,* by Alan Paton. Copyright © 1968, 1982 by The Seabury Press, Inc. Reprinted by permission of Harper Collins Publishers.

The prayers of Arthur A. Rouner, Jr. (Aug. 17; Sept. 24; Oct. 12; Dec. 26) are from *Someone's Praying, Lord,* copyright © 1970 by Arthur A. Rouner. Used by permission of Arthur A. Rouner.

The prayers of Robert C. Savage (May 2; June 7; July 22; Aug. 21; Sept. 16; Nov. 20) are from *Pocket Praise,* published by Tyndale House Publishers, Inc., copyright © 1985 by Robert C. Savage. Used by permission of Tyndale House Publishers, Inc.

Table of Contents

Publisher's Note

THE ONE YEAR BOOK OF PERSONAL PRAYER
has been prepared to help you in the discipline
of daily prayer. It is an ideal starting point both
for private and family devotions. The selections
for each day include a portion from the Psalms,
a selected prayer, and a short inspirational quote
emphasizing an important aspect of prayer.
Author and Scripture indexes are provided to
help you locate and review prayers and quotes
that especially speak to you.

The outdated pronouns of some older prayers
have been changed from *thee, thou,* and *thy* to
the more contemporary *you* and *your,* making
the prayers easier for most contemporary
readers to read and understand. Plural pronouns
in some corporate prayers have been changed to
the singular forms, creating a more personal
quality. Prayers altered in these ways are
identified as having been "adapted" from the
original. Some portions of Scripture have been
modified just enough to fit the form of a
personal prayer and are also shown to be
"adapted."

Over the ages, innumerable prayers have been
spoken from the lips of humanity to the listening

ears of God. The prayers gathered in this book are among the relatively few that have been recorded and passed along to the present day. They are the words of a wide variety of authors. Some are well known, like the apostle Paul and Pat Boone. Others will never be known, like a fallen Confederate soldier and an unknown Chinese woman. Some of the prayers are as ancient as the Old Testament and others are so new they were written especially for this volume.

It is important to remember that these prayers are not replacements for the expression of your own heart's desire toward God. Rather, they are inspirational guides to lead you into the practice of personal daily prayer. Their words should serve as fuel to fire your own prayers, praises, and thanksgivings. They should cheer you and encourage you to lighten your lives every day by drawing near to God. We pray that your lives will be enriched, this year and every year, by a growing intimacy with God through regular personal prayer.

Blessed is the man who does not walk in the counsel of the wicked or stand in the way of sinners or sit in the seat of mockers.   PSALM 1:1

*E*TERNAL GOD, you make all things new, and abide for ever the same: grant me to begin this year in your faith, and to continue it in your favor, that, being guided in all my doings, and guarded all my days, I may spend my life in your service, and finally, by your grace, attain the glory of everlasting life, through Jesus Christ my Lord.   W. E. ORCHARD (adapted)

When you pray, rather let your heart be without words than your words without heart.

JOHN BUNYAN

*Therefore, you kings, be wise; be warned, you
rulers of the earth. Serve the LORD with fear and
rejoice with trembling.*   PSALM 2:10-11

O LORD GOD, Holy Father, . . . I am no
longer my own, but Thine. Put me to
what Thou wilt, rank me with whom
Thou wilt; put me to doing, put me to suffering;
let me be employed for Thee or laid aside for
Thee, exalted for Thee or brought low for Thee;
let me be full, let me be empty; let me have all
things, let me have nothing; I freely and heartily
yield all things to Thy pleasure and disposal.

And now, O glorious and blessed God, Father,
Son, and Holy Spirit, Thou art mine, and I am
Thine. So be it. And the Covenant which I have
made on earth, let it be ratified in heaven.

METHODIST SHORTER BOOK OF OFFICES

*In prayer the lips ne'er act the winning part,
Without the sweet concurrence of the heart.*
ROBERT HERRICK

Many are saying of me, "God will not deliver him."
But you are a shield around me, O LORD; you
bestow glory on me and lift up my head.

PSALM 3:2-3

BLESSING and honor, thanksgiving
                    and praise
          more than we can utter be unto you,
O most adorable Trinity, Father, Son,
          and Holy Ghost,
by all angels, all men, all creatures
for ever and ever. Amen and amen.
To God the Father, who first loved us,
and made us accepted in the beloved;
to God the Son who loved us,
and washed us from our sins in his own blood;
to God the Holy Ghost,
who sheds the love of God abroad in our hearts
be all love and all glory for time and for eternity.
Amen.   THOMAS KEN

I have lived to thank God that all my prayers have
not been answered.   JEAN INGELOW

Know that the LORD has set apart the godly for himself; the LORD will hear when I call to him.

PSALM 4:3

I BIND unto myself today
The power of God to hold and lead,
His eye to watch, his might to stay,
His ear to hearken to my need.
The wisdom of my God to teach,
His hand to guide, his shield to ward;
The word of God to give me speech,
His heavenly host to be my guard.

I bind unto myself the name,
The strong name of the Trinity;
By invocation of the same,
The Three in One, the One in Three,
Of whom all nature hath creation;
Eternal Father, Spirit, Word,
Praise to the Lord of my salvation,
Salvation is of Christ the Lord.

PATRICK OF IRELAND

If Christians spent as much time praying as they do grumbling, they would soon have nothing to grumble about.   ANONYMOUS

Listen to my cry for help, my King and my God, for to you I pray. In the morning, O LORD, you hear my voice; in the morning I lay my requests before you and wait in expectation.   PSALM 5:2-3

GIVE ME, O Lord, a steadfast heart, which no unworthy affection may drag downwards; give me an unconquered heart, which no tribulation can wear out; give me an upright heart, which no unworthy purpose may tempt aside. Bestow on me also, O Lord my God, understanding to know you, diligence to seek you, wisdom to find you, and a faithfulness that may finally embrace you, through Jesus Christ our Lord. Amen.

THOMAS AQUINAS

He who aims at inward and spiritual things must, with Jesus, turn aside from the crowd.

THOMAS À KEMPIS

*Be merciful to me, L*ORD*, for I am faint; O L*ORD*, heal me, for my bones are in agony. . . . Turn, O L*ORD*, and deliver me; save me because of your unfailing love.*   PSALM 6:2, 4

ALMIGHTY GOD, Lord of the storm and of the calm, the vexed sea and the quiet haven, of day and of night, of life and of death, grant unto us so to have our hearts stayed upon your faithfulness, your unchangingness and love, that, whatsoever betide us, however black the cloud or dark the night, with quiet faith trusting in you we may look upon you with untroubled eye, and walking in lowliness toward you, and in lovingness toward another, abide all storms and troubles of this mortal life, begging you that they may turn to the soul's true good. We ask it for your mercy's sake, shown in Jesus Christ our Lord.   GEORGE DAWSON

The prayer of faith is the only power in the universe to which the great Jehovah yields.   ROBERT HALL

Let the assembled peoples gather around you. Rule over them from on high; let the LORD judge the peoples. Judge me, O LORD, according to my righteousness, according to my integrity, O Most High.   PSALM 7:7-8

GLORIOUS GOD, give me grace to amend my life, and to have an eye to my end without begrudging death, which to those who die in you, good Lord, is the gate of a wealthy life.

Give me, good Lord, a full faith, a firm hope, and a fervent charity, a love of you incomparably above the love of myself.

Give me, good Lord, a longing to be with you, not to avoid the calamities of this world, not so much to attain the joys of heaven, as simply for love of you.

And give me, good Lord, your love and favor, which my love of you, however great it might be, could not deserve were it not for your great goodness.

These things, good Lord, that I pray for, give me your grace to labor for.   THOMAS MORE

O Lord, let me not live to be useless!
                          BISHOP JOHN DE STRATFORD

Lord, our Lord, how majestic is your name in all the earth! You have set your glory above the heavens. From the lips of children and infants you have ordained praise.   PSALM 8:1-2

BEHOLD, Lord, an empty vessel that needs to be filled. My Lord, fill it. I am weak in the faith; strengthen me. I am cold in love; warm me and make me fervent, that my love may go out to my neighbor. I do not have a strong and firm faith; at times I doubt and am unable to trust you altogether. O Lord, help me. Strengthen my faith and trust in you. In you I have sealed the treasure of all I have. I am poor; you are rich and came to be merciful to the poor. I am a sinner; you are upright. With me, there is an abundance of sin; in you is the fullness of righteousness. Therefore I will remain with you, of whom I can receive, but to whom I may not give.

MARTIN LUTHER

It is good for us to keep some account of our prayers, that we may not unsay them in our practice.   MATTHEW HENRY

*I will praise you, O LORD, with all my heart; I will
tell of all your wonders. I will be glad and rejoice in
you; I will sing praise to your name, O Most High.*

PSALM 9:1-2

USE ME THEN, my Savior, for whatever
purpose, and in whatever way, you
may require. Here is my poor heart, an
empty vessel; fill it with your grace. Here is my
sinful and troubled soul; quicken it and refresh
it with your love. Take my heart for your abode;
my mouth to spread abroad the glory of your
name; my love and all my powers, for the
advancement of your believing people; and
never suffer the steadfastness and confidence of
my faith to abate; so that at all times I may be
enabled from the heart to say, "Jesus needs me,
and I am his."   DWIGHT L. MOODY

*When you go to your knees, God will help you
stand up to anything.*   ANONYMOUS

Arise, O LORD, let not man triumph; let the nations be judged in your presence. Strike them with terror, O LORD; let the nations know they are but men.

PSALM 9:19-20

O GOD, ever blessed, who hast given me the night for rest and the day for labor and service, grant that the refreshing sleep of the night now past may be turned to Thy greater glory in the life of the day now before me. Let it breed no slothfulness within me, but rather send me to more diligent action and more willing obedience. Teach me, O God, so to use all the circumstances of my life today that they may bring forth in me the fruits of holiness rather than the fruits of sin.   JOHN BAILLIE

For each new morning with its light,
For rest and shelter of the night,
For health and food, for love and friends,
For everything Thy goodness sends.

RALPH WALDO EMERSON

Arise, LORD! Lift up your hand, O God. Do not
forget the helpless.   PSALM 10:12

G IVE us courage, O Lord, to stand up
           and be counted,
     to stand up for those who cannot stand
        up for themselves,
to stand up for ourselves when it is needful for
        us to do so.
Let us fear nothing more than we fear you.
Let us love nothing more that we love you,
for thus we shall fear nothing also.
Let us have no other God before you,
whether nation or party or state or church.
Let us seek no other peace but the peace
           which is yours,
and make us its instruments,
opening our eyes and our ears and our hearts,
so that we should know always what work of
           peace we may do for you.

                                              ALAN PATON

Keep us, Lord, so awake in the duties of our calling
that we may sleep in thy peace and wake in thy
glory.   JOHN DONNE

*The LORD is King for ever and ever; the nations will
perish from his land. You hear, O LORD, the desire of
the afflicted; you encourage them, and you listen to
their cry.*   PSALM 10:16-17

DEAR GOD, you are the heavenly Father.
I am a father too, but I am earthly. One
small family has come out from me and
bears my name, yet, in truth, every family in
heaven and earth takes its name from you. So I
pray that you would care for this family because
of your holy name. Give them what only a
heavenly Father can give. That is, just as I gave
them their first birth on earth, you would give
them a second birth from heaven. I ask you this
because I know that it is only in this way that
they can have the eternal life you promised in
your beloved Son, Jesus Christ our Lord. Amen.

DANIEL PARTNER

*Prayer, in its simplest definition, is merely a wish
turned God-ward.*   PHILLIPS BROOKS

The LORD is in his holy temple; the LORD is on his heavenly throne. He observes the sons of men; his eyes examine them.   PSALM 11:4

O LORD GOD, whose will it is that, next to yourself, we should hold our parents in highest honor; it is not the least of our duties to beseech your goodness towards them. Preserve, I pray, my parents and home, in the love of your religion and in health of body and mind. Grant that through me no sorrow may befall them; and finally, as they are kind to me, so may you be to them, O supreme Father of all.

DESIDERIUS ERASMUS

Religion is no more possible without prayer than poetry without language or music without atmosphere.   JAMES MARTINEAU

Help, LORD, for the godly are no more; the faithful have vanished from among men. Everyone lies to his neighbor; their flattering lips speak with deception. . . . "Because of the oppression of the weak and the groaning of the needy, I will now arise," says the LORD.   PSALM 12:1-2, 5

*O*UR FATHER, You come seeking fruit. Teach me, I pray You, to realize how truly this is the one object of my existence, and of my union to Christ. Make it the one desire of my heart to be a branch, so filled with the Spirit of the Vine, as to bring forth fruit abundantly.   ANDREW MURRAY (adapted)

Take my will, and make it Thine,
  It shall be no longer mine;
Take my heart, it is Thine own;
  It shall be Thy royal throne.
                    FRANCES R. HAVERGAL

*Look on me and answer, O LORD my God. Give light
to my eyes, or I will sleep in death.*   PSALM 13:3

I BOW my knees before you Father, from
whom every family in heaven and on earth
takes its name. I pray that, according to the
riches of your glory, you may grant that I may be
strengthened in my inner being with power
through your Spirit, and that Christ may dwell
in my heart through faith, as I am being rooted
and grounded in love. I pray that I may have the
power to comprehend, with all the saints, what
is the breadth and length and height and depth,
and to know the love of Christ that surpasses
knowledge, so that I may be filled with all the
fullness of God.   EPHESIANS 3:14-19 (adapted)

*We ought to act with God in the greatest simplicity,
speaking to Him frankly and plainly, and imploring
His assistance in our affairs, just as they happen.*
                                    BROTHER LAWRENCE

Oh, that salvation for Israel would come out of Zion! When the LORD restores the fortunes of his people, let Jacob rejoice and Israel be glad!

PSALM 14:7

WE THANK YOU, O Lord our God, for all Your goodness. You have shielded, rescued, helped and guided us all the days of our lives, and brought us unto this hour. Grant in Your goodness that we may spend this day without sin, in joy and reverence of You. Drive away from us all envy, all fear. Bestow upon us what is good and meet. And lead us not into temptation, but deliver us from evil.   ANONYMOUS

In seasons of distress and grief,
  My soul has often found relief,
And oft escaped the tempter's snare,
  By thy return, sweet hour of prayer.

W. W. WALFORD

LORD, who may dwell in your sanctuary? Who may live on your holy hill? He whose walk is blameless and who does what is righteous, who speaks the truth from his heart.   PSALM 15:1-2

WE THANK THEE, Lord, that however hopeless our work may seem, however dark the night around us, however meager the response to Thy Spirit, still Thou hast ordained for us a hope.

We thank Thee that we can never despair because we know, past all doubting, that here and there in this world Thy kingdom has already come, Thy will has already begun to rule.

We thank Thee that here and there are homes made beautiful by Thy presence, lives lived purely and faithfully for Thee, children and child-like souls whose clear and simple trust brings Thee Thyself down amongst men.

J. S. HOWLAND

Prayer opens our eyes that we may see ourselves and others as God sees us.   CLARA PALMER

Keep me safe, O God, for in you I take refuge. I said to the LORD, *"You are my Lord; apart from you I have no good thing."*   PSALM 16:1-2

O LORD, Jesus Christ,
    who is as the shadow of a great rock in
        a weary land,
who beholds your weak creatures
weary of labor, weary of pleasure,
weary of hope deferred, weary of self;
in your abundant compassion,
and fellow feeling with us,
and unutterable tenderness,
bring us, we pray you,
into your rest.   CHRISTINA ROSSETTI

There is no life that is not in community,
And no community not lived in praise of God.
                                        T. S. ELIOT

Show the wonder of your great love, you who save by your right hand those who take refuge in you from their foes. Keep me as the apple of your eye; hide me in the shadow of your wings.

PSALM 17:7-8

THANKS be to you, Lord Jesus Christ, for all the benefits which you have won for us, for all the pains and insults which you have borne for us. O most merciful Redeemer, Friend and Brother, may we know you more clearly, love you more dearly, and follow you more nearly, day by day.

RICHARD OF CHICHESTER

More things are wrought by prayer than this world dreams of. ALFRED LORD TENNYSON

*I love you, O LORD, my strength. The LORD is my
rock, my fortress and my deliverer; my God is my
rock, in whom I take refuge. He is my shield and the
horn of my salvation, my stronghold.*

PSALM 18:1-2

MORNING AND EVENING I commit
my soul to Jesus Christ, the Savior of
the world. Enable me, O God, to
observe what He says to me: resolutely to obey
His precepts and endeavor to follow His example
in those things wherein He is exhibited to us as a
pattern for our imitation. Make plain to me that
no circumstance nor time of life can occur but I
may find something either spoken by our Lord
Himself or by His Spirit in the prophets or
apostles that will direct my conduct, if I am but
faithful to You and my own soul. Amen.

SUSANNA WESLEY

*Ask, and it shall be given you; seek, and ye shall
find; knock, and it shall be opened unto you.*

MATTHEW 7:7, *KJV*

He reached down from on high and took hold of me;
he drew me out of deep waters. He rescued me from
my powerful enemy, from my foes, who were too
strong for me.   PSALM 18:16-17

COME, Therefore, O Lord Jesus, divest
yourself of your garments which you
have put on for my sake. Be naked, that
you may clothe us with your mercy. Gird yourself
with a towel for our sakes, that you may gird us
with your gift of immortality. Pour water into the
basin; wash not only our feet but also the head,
and not only the footprints of the body, but also of
the mind. I wish to put off all the filth of my
frailty, so that I, too, may say: "I have put off my gar-
ment, how shall I put it on? I have washed my
feet, how shall I defile them?"   AMBROSE

Rejoice always, pray constantly, and in all circum-
stances give thanks.   THE DESERT FATHERS

The LORD lives! Praise be to my Rock! Exalted be
God my Savior.   PSALM 18:46

O LORD:
Keep me from vain strife or words:
Grant to me a constant
Profession of the truth!
Preserve me in the faith,
True faith and undefiled,
That ever I may hold fast
That which I professed when I was baptized
Unto, and in the name of,
Father,
The Son,
The Holy Ghost—
That I may have you for my Father,
That in your Son I may abide,
And in the fellowship of the Holy Ghost:
Through the same Jesus Christ,
Our Lord. Amen.   HILARY OF POITIERS (adapted)

Deep down in me I knowed it was a lie, and He
knowed it. You can't pray a lie—I found that out.
                              MARK TWAIN, *Huck Finn*

The heavens declare the glory of God; the skies proclaim the work of his hands. Day after day they pour forth speech; night after night they display knowledge.   PSALM 19:1-2

O LORD and Saviour Christ, who comes not to strive nor cry, but to let your words fall as the drops that water the earth; grant all who contend for the faith once delivered, never to injure it by clamour and impatience; but speaking your precious truth in love so to present it that it may be loved, and that men may see in it your goodness and your beauty.

WILLIAM BRIGHT

Let me depend on God alone:
    who never changes,
    who knows what is best for me so much better
        than I;
and gives in a thousand ways, at all times
    all that the perfect Father can for the son's good
        growth,
    things needful, things salutary,
    things wise, beneficent and happy.

ERIC MILNER-WHITE

May the LORD *answer you when you are in distress;*
may the name of the God of Jacob protect you. May
he send you help from the sanctuary and grant you
support from Zion.   PSALM 20:1-2

*B*E OFF, Satan, from this door and from
these four walls. This is no place for you;
there is nothing for you to do here. This
is the place for Peter and Paul and the holy
gospel; and this is where I mean to sleep, now
that my worship is done, in the name of the
Father and of the Holy Spirit.

In the name of our Lord Jesus Christ, send me
your Spirit; instill the wisdom of your Holy
Spirit into my heart; protect my soul and body,
every limb in my body, every fiber of my being,
from all possible harm and all traps the Devil
may set for me and every temptation to sin.

EUCHOLOGIUM SINAITICUM

O what peace we often forfeit,
O what needless pain we bear,
All because we do not carry
Everything to God in prayer!   JOSEPH SCRIVEN

O Lord, the king rejoices in your strength. How great is his joy in the victories you give! You have granted him the desire of his heart and have not withheld the request of his lips.   PSALM 21:1-2

I CALL upon you, O LORD; come quickly to me;
    give ear to my voice when I call to you.
  Let my prayer be counted as incense before you,
and the lifting up of my hands as an evening
    sacrifice.

Set a guard over my mouth, O LORD;
    keep watch over the door of my lips.
Do not turn my heart to any evil,
    to busy myself with wicked deeds
in company with those who work iniquity;
    do not let me eat of their delicacies.

                              PSALM 141:1-4, NRSV

God eagerly awaits the chance to bless the person whose heart is turned toward Him.   ANONYMOUS

Yet you are enthroned as the Holy One; you are the praise of Israel. In you our fathers put their trust; they trusted and you delivered them.   PSALM 22:3-4

O LORD GOD, when you give to your servants to endeavor any great matter, grant us also to know that it is not the beginning, but the continuing of the same to the end, until it be thoroughly finished, which yields the true glory; through him who for the finishing of your work laid down his life, our Redeemer, Jesus Christ.   FRANCIS DRAKE

Pray, always pray; though weary, faint, and lone, Prayer nestles by the Father's sheltering throne.
A. B. SIMPSON

You who fear the LORD, praise him! All you descendants of Jacob, honor him! Revere him, all you descendants of Israel!   PSALM 22:23

WHO CAN TELL what a day may bring forth? Cause me therefore, gracious God, to live every day as if it were to be my last, for I know not but that it may be such. Cause me to live now as I shall wish I had done when I come to die. O grant that I may not die with any guilt on my conscience, or any known sin unrepented of, but that I may be found in Christ, who is my only Saviour and Redeemer.   THOMAS À KEMPIS

Prayer should be the key of the day and the lock of the night.   THOMAS FULLER

The LORD is my shepherd, I shall lack nothing. He makes me lie down in green pastures, he leads me beside quiet waters, he restores my soul.

PSALM 23:1-3

*L*ORD, behold our family here assembled. We thank you for this place in which we dwell, for the love that unites us, for the peace accorded us this day, for the hope with which we expect the morrow; for the health, the work, the food, and the bright skies that make our lives delightful; for our friends in all parts of the earth.

Bless us, if it may be, in all our innocent endeavors; if it may not, give us the strength to endure that which is to come that we may be brave in peril, constant in tribulation, temperate in wrath, and in all changes of fortune, and down to the gates of death, loyal and loving to one another.

As the clay to the potter, as the windmill to the wind, as children of their sire, we beseech of you this help and mercy for Christ's sake.

ROBERT LOUIS STEVENSON

Our thanks to God should always precede our requests.   ANONYMOUS

Who may ascend the hill of the LORD? Who may stand in his holy place? He who has clean hands and a pure heart, who does not lift up his soul to an idol or swear by what is false.   PSALM 24:3-4

O LORD our God, even at this moment as we come blundering into Thy presence in prayer, we are haunted by memories of duties unperformed, promptings disobeyed, and beckonings ignored. Opportunities to be kind knocked on the door of our hearts and went weeping away. We are ashamed, O Lord, and tired of failure.

If Thou art drawing close to us now, come nearer still, till selfishness is burned out within us and our wills lose their weakness in union with Thine own. Amen.   PETER MARSHALL

They tell about a fifteen-year-old boy in an orphans' home who had an incurable stutter. One Sunday the minister was detained and the boy volunteered to say the prayer in his stead. He did it perfectly, too, without a single stutter. Later he explained, "I don't stutter when I talk to God. He loves me."

                                                    BENNETT CERF

Show me your ways, O LORD, teach me your paths;
guide me in your truth and teach me, for you are
God my Savior, and my hope is in you all day long.

PSALM 25:4-5

O THOU, who art the Light of the minds that know Thee, and the Life of the souls that love Thee, and the Strength of the thoughts that seek Thee; help us so to know Thee that we may truly love Thee; so to love Thee that we may truly serve Thee, whose service is perfect freedom; through Jesus Christ our Lord. Amen.

GELASIAN SACRAMENTARY

There is nothing that makes us love a man so much
as praying for him.   WILLIAM LAW

*Turn to me and be gracious to me, for I am lonely
and afflicted. The troubles of my heart have
multiplied; free me from my anguish.*

PSALM 25:16-17

*L*ORD, you know better than I know
myself that I am growing older, and will
someday be old. Keep me from getting
talkative, and particularly from the fatal habit of
thinking that I must say something on every
subject and on every occasion.

I ask for grace enough to listen to the tales of
others' pains. But seal my lips on my own aches
and pains; help me to endure them with
patience.

Give me the ability to see good things in
unexpected places, and talents in unexpected
people. And give me, O Lord, the grace to tell
them so.   ANONYMOUS

*We must lay before him what is in us, not what
ought to be in us.*   C. S. LEWIS

Test me, O LORD, and try me, examine my heart and my mind; for your love is ever before me, and I walk continually in your truth.   PSALM 26:2-3

O LORD, you are my redemption, also be my protector; direct my mind by your gracious presence, and watch over my path with guiding love; that, among the snares which lie hidden in this path in which I walk, I may so pass onwards with my heart fixed on you, that by the track of faith I may come to be where you would have me.

MOZARABIC SACRAMENTARY

God showed Abraham that asking for anything is allowed with the understanding that God's answers come from God's perspective. They are not always in harmony with our expectations, for only he knows the whole story.

LIFE APPLICATION BIBLE on Genesis 18:33

The LORD is my light and my salvation—whom shall I fear? The LORD is the stronghold of my life—of whom shall I be afraid?   PSALM 27:1

*F*ATHER ALMIGHTY, who are not served by men's hands as though you need anything, but who delights in the worship of a contrite heart, grant us grace in this hour of worship to forswear the pride to which our hearts are prone, to remember that you have made us and not we ourselves, that you are the beginning and the end of our life. Grant us to know the limit of our knowledge that we may seek your wisdom, and to know the limit of our power so that we may glory in your strength which is made perfect in weakness. So may we worship you in humility, and arise to newness of life by fellowship with you. Amen.

REINHOLD NIEBUHR

Help me to work and pray,
  Help me to live each day,
That all I do may say,
  Thy kingdom come.   A. B. SIMPSON

Hear my voice when I call, O LORD; be merciful to me and answer me. My heart says of you, "Seek his face!" Your face, LORD, I will seek.   PSALM 27:7-8

O LORD JESUS CHRIST, you have said that you are the way, the truth, and the life. Suffer us not to stray from you, who are the way, nor to distrust you who are the truth, nor to rest in anything other than you, who are the life.   DESIDERIUS ERASMUS

There are two main pitfalls on the road to mastery of the art of prayer. If a person gets what he asks for, his humility is in danger. If he fails to get what he asks for, he is apt to lose confidence. Indeed, no matter whether prayer seems to be succeeding or failing, humility and confidence are two virtues which are absolutely essential.   A TRAPPIST MONK

*Praise be to the L*ORD*, for he has heard my cry for mercy. The L*ORD *is my strength and my shield; my heart trusts in him, and I am helped.*   PSALM 28:6-7

SO MUCH of the world goes to bed hungry every night, but we are blessed with abundance. The bellies of Third World children swell through malnutrition, but the only way our bellies swell is through overeating. We wonder what God's plan on this earth must be. Help us, O Lord, to an awareness of our spiritual and physical needs, and of the needs of people in all countries of this world—as we give thanks for the food that is set before us. Amen.

PAUL SIMPSON MCELROY

Our Father, let the spirit of gratitude so prevail in our hearts that we may manifest thy Spirit in our lives.   W. B. SLACK

Ascribe to the LORD, *O mighty ones, ascribe to the* LORD
glory and strength. Ascribe to the LORD *the glory
due his name; worship the* LORD *in the splendor of
his holiness.*   PSALM 29:1-2

FATHER, I am beginning to know how much I miss when I fail to talk to thee in prayer, and through prayer to receive into my life the strength and the guidance which only thou canst give. Forgive me for the pride and the presumption that make me continue to struggle to manage my own affairs to the exhaustion of my body, the weariness of my mind, the trial of my faith.

Let not, I pray, any future forgetfulness of mine, or a false sense of self-sufficiency, any spiritual laziness, or doubt of thy faithfulness keep me from taking everything to thee in prayer.

And now, I thank thee that the fresh breath of heaven is even now blowing away the close, damp air of all my failure, of every doubt and fear. I ask thee for that soul tonic of prayer that shall reburnish my faith, brighten my hope, revive and rekindle my love. In thy name, I pray. Amen.

PETER MARSHALL

*Lord, you know how busy I must be this day. If I
forget you, do not you forget me.*   JACOB ASTLEY

Sing to the LORD, you saints of his; praise his holy name. For his anger lasts only a moment, but his favor lasts a lifetime; weeping may remain for a night, but rejoicing comes in the morning.

PSALM 30:4-5

*L*ORD JESUS CHRIST, who stretched out your hands on the cross, and redeemed us by your blood: forgive me, a sinner, for none of my thoughts are hid from you. Pardon I ask, pardon I hope for, pardon I trust to have. You who are full of pity and mercy: spare me, and forgive.   AMBROSE

Have we trials and temptations?
  Is there trouble anywhere?
We should never be discouraged,
    Take it to the Lord in prayer.   JOSEPH SCRIVEN

In you, O LORD, I have taken refuge; let me never be put to shame; deliver me in your righteousness. Turn your ear to me, come quickly to my rescue; be my rock of refuge, a strong fortress to save me.

PSALM 31:1-2

JESUS, my feet are dirty. Come and slave for me; pour your water into your basin and come and wash my feet. I am over bold, I know, in asking this, but I dread what you threatened when you said: "If I do not wash your feet, it means you have no companionship with me." Wash my feet, then, because I do want to have companionship with you. And yet, why am I saying: "Wash my feet"? It was all very well for Peter to say that, for in his case all that needed washing was his feet: he was clean through and through. My position is quite different: you may wash me now, but I shall still need that other washing you were thinking of, Lord, when you said: "There is a baptism I must needs be baptized with."   ORIGEN OF ALEXANDRIA

For food, for raiment, for life and opportunity, for sun and rain, for water and the portage trails, we give you thanks, O Lord.

A PRAYER FROM THE NORTH WOODS

*Be merciful to me, O LORD, for I am in distress; my
eyes grow weak with sorrow, my soul and my body
with grief.*   PSALM 31:9

*H*ELPER of men who turn to you,
    Light of men in the dark,
    Creator of all that grows from seed,
Promoter of all spiritual growth,
have mercy, Lord, on me
and make me a temple fit for yourself.
Do not scan my transgressions too closely,
for if you are quick to notice my offenses,
I shall not dare to appear before you.
In your great mercy,
in your boundless compassion,
wash away my sins, through Jesus Christ,
your only Child, the truly holy,
the chief of our souls' healers.
Through him may all glory be given you,
all power and honor and praise,
throughout the ending succession of ages.
Amen.   BERLIN PAPYRUS

*Who rises from prayer a better man, his prayer is
answered.*   GEORGE MEREDITH

*How great is your goodness, which you have stored
up for those who fear you, which you bestow in the
sight of men on those who take refuge in you.*

PSALM 31:19

*L*ET us not seek out of you what we can
only find in you, O Lord.
Peace and rest and joy and bliss,
which abide only in your abiding joy.
Lift up our souls above the weary fount of
harassing thoughts to your eternal
presence.
Lift up our minds to the pure, bright serene
atmosphere of your presence,
that we may breathe freely,
there repose in your love,
there be at rest from ourselves
and from all things that weary us:
and then return, arrayed in thy peace,
to do and to bear
whatsoever shall best please you, O blessed
Lord. E. B. PUSEY

*We do pray for mercy, and that same prayer doth
teach us all to render the deeds of mercy.*

WILLIAM SHAKESPEARE, *Merchant of Venice*

Blessed is he whose transgressions are forgiven,
whose sins are covered. Blessed is the man whose
sin the LORD does not count against him and in
whose spirit is no deceit.   PSALM 32:1-2

O GOD, make the door of this house wide
enough to receive all who need human
love and fellowship; narrow enough to
shut out all envy, pride, and strife.

Make its threshold smooth enough to be no
stumbling block to children nor to straying feet,
but rugged and strong enough to turn back the
tempter's power. God, make the door of this
house the gateway to thine eternal kingdom.

On ST. STEPHEN'S WALLBROOK, LONDON

And now unto him who is able to keep us from
falling and lift us from the dark valley of despair to
the bright mountain of hope, from the midnight of
desperation to the daybreak of joy; to him be power
and authority, for ever and ever.

MARTIN LUTHER KING, JR.

Sing joyfully to the LORD, you righteous; it is fitting for the upright to praise him. Praise the LORD with the harp; make music to him on the ten-stringed lyre.

PSALM 33:1-2

O LORD GOD, I am learning that I can do nothing apart from your Holy Spirit. Your Spirit lifts me up in prayer. Your Spirit prepares my heart for prayer. Your Spirit aids me in resting my heart and mind in you in prayer. Your Spirit prompts me to pray for the things of your heart, and he leads me beyond selfish desires. May I be continually inspired by your Spirit to say and do and pray consistently, that my life might be a witness to others regarding the blessed power of prayer and your work through your Spirit. Amen.

LOUIS GIFFORD PARKHURST, JR.

Prayer is an end to isolation. It is living our daily life with someone; with him who alone can deliver us from solitude.   GEORGES LEFEVRE

From heaven the LORD looks down and sees all mankind; from his dwelling place he watches all who live on earth—he who forms the hearts of all, who considers everything they do.   PSALM 33:13-15

FATHER, when your Son Jesus Christ prayed, he looked up to heaven and spoke to you, so now I follow his example. I will confidently speak with you as a man on earth to his God in heaven.

Your kingdom is in heaven, O God, but my feet stand on earth and my eyes look up in prayer. Father, I ask you, bring your kingdom to earth. Just as John looked up and saw the holy city, the New Jerusalem, coming down out of heaven, I pray that my eyes would see the coming of your kingdom. Just as he heard the voice from the throne, so may I hear the voices at the seventh trumpet proclaim, "The kingdom of the world has become the kingdom of our Lord and of his Christ, and he will reign forever and ever." Amen.

DANIEL PARTNER

O Christ my Lord and King,
This is the prayer I bring,
This is the song I sing,
Thy kingdom come.   A. B. SIMPSON

*The angel of the LORD encamps around those who
fear him, and he delivers them. Taste and see that
the LORD is good; blessed is the man who takes
refuge in him.*   PSALM 34:7-8

W E BEG YOU, Lord, to help and defend us. Deliver the oppressed, pity
the insignificant, raise the fallen,
show yourself to the needy, heal the sick, bring
back those of your people who have gone astray,
feed the hungry, lift up the weak, take off the
prisoner's chains. May every nation come to
know that you alone are God, that Jesus Christ is
your Child, that we are your people, the sheep
that you pasture.   CLEMENT OF ROME

Restraining prayer, we cease to fight;
Prayer keeps the Christian's armor bright;
And Satan trembles when he sees
The weakest saint upon his knees.
                                        WILLIAM COWPER

The righteous cry out, and the LORD hears them; he delivers them from all their troubles. The LORD is close to the brokenhearted and saves those who are crushed in spirit.   PSALM 34:17-18

O LORD, you are never weary of doing me good. Let me never be weary of doing you service. But as you have pleasure in the prosperity of your servants, so let me take pleasure in the service of my Lord, and abound in your work, and in your love and praise evermore. O fill up all that is wanting, reform whatever is amiss in me, perfect the thing that concerns me. Let the witness of your pardoning love ever abide in my heart.

JOHN WESLEY (adapted)

The right way to pray, then, is any way that allows us to communicate with God. For prayer is not a ritual; it is the soul's inherent response to a relationship with a loving Father.

COLLEEN TOWNSEND EVANS

My soul will rejoice in the LORD and delight in his salvation. My whole being will exclaim, "Who is like you, O LORD? You rescue the poor from those too strong for them, the poor and needy from those who rob them."   PSALM 35:9-10

MAY NONE of God's wonderful works keep silence, night or morning. Bright stars, high mountains, the depths of the seas, sources of rushing rivers: may all these break into song as I sing to Father, Son, and Holy Spirit. May all the angels in the heavens reply: Amen, Amen, Amen. Power, praise, honor, eternal glory to God, the only giver of grace, Amen, Amen, Amen.   ANONYMOUS

O Lord, heavenly Father, in whom is the fullness of light and wisdom, enlighten our minds by your Holy Spirit, and give us grace to receive your Word with reverence and humility, without which no one can understand your truth. For Christ's sake, amen.
                                    JOHN CALVIN

*O LORD, how long will you look on? Rescue my life
from their ravages, my precious life from these
lions. I will give you thanks in the great assembly;
among throngs of people I will praise you.*

PSALM 35:17-18

ALMIGHTY,
   forgive my doubt,
      my anger,
my pride.
By your mercy abase me,
in your strictness
raise me up.

DAG HAMMARSKJÖLD, *Mercy and Justice*

*Joshua poured out his real thoughts to God. Hiding
your needs from God is ignoring the only one who
can really help. Any believer can become more
honest in prayer by remembering that God is
all-knowing and all-powerful.*

LIFE APPLICATION BIBLE *on Joshua 7:7-9*

Your love, O LORD, reaches to the heavens, your faithfulness to the skies. Your righteousness is like the mighty mountains, your justice like the great deep.   PSALM 36:5-6

GOD of all grace, give me your peace that passes understanding, the quietness that comes from friendliness with human beings, and may true divine friendship with you possess my soul; that I, withdrawn awhile from the turmoil of the world, may gather the strength that I have lost, and established and strengthened by your grace, pass on through all the troubles of this my earthly life, safe into the haven of eternal rest; through Jesus Christ my Lord. Amen.   GEORGE DAWSON

The first purpose of prayer is to know God.
                                              CHARLES L. ALLEN

Trust in the LORD and do good; dwell in the land and enjoy safe pasture. Delight yourself in the LORD and he will give you the desires of your heart.

PSALM 37:3-4

O MY LORD, you have said, "Ask for whatever you wish and it will be done for you." Why is it that my heart is so little able to accept these words in their divine simplicity? Oh, help me to see that what I need is nothing less than this promise to overcome the powers of the world and Satan! Teach me to pray in the faith of this Thy promise.

ANDREW MURRAY (adapted)

If ye abide in me, and my words abide in you, ye shall ask what ye will, and it shall be done unto you.

JOHN 15:7, KJV

If the LORD delights in a man's way, he makes his steps firm; though he stumble, he will not fall, for the LORD upholds him with his hand.

PSALM 37:23-24

GRACIOUS and holy Father, give me wisdom to perceive you, intelligence to fathom you, patience to wait for you, eyes to behold you, a heart to meditate upon you, and a life to proclaim you, through the power of the Spirit of Jesus Christ our Lord.

BENEDICT

Prayer covers the whole of a man's life. There is no thought, feeling, yearning, or desire, however low, trifling, or vulgar we may deem it, which, if it affects our real interest or happiness, we may not lay before God and be sure of sympathy. His nature is such that our often coming does not tire him. The whole burden of the whole life of every man may be rolled on to God and not weary him, though it has wearied the man. HENRY WARD BEECHER

The mouth of the righteous man utters wisdom, and his tongue speaks what is just. The law of his God is in his heart; his feet do not slip.

PSALM 37:30-31

ALMIGHTY GOD, our heavenly Father, without whose help labour is useless, without whose light search is vain, invigorate my studies and establish myself and others in your holy Faith. Take not, O Lord, your Holy Spirit from me, let not evil thoughts have dominion in my mind. Let me not linger in ignorance and doubt, but enlighten and support me for the sake of Jesus Christ our Lord. Amen.

SAMUEL JOHNSON

The cry of a young raven is nothing but the natural cry of a creature, but your cry, if it be sincere, is the result of a work of grace in your heart.

CHARLES H. SPURGEON

O LORD, do not forsake me; be not far from me, O my God. Come quickly to help me, O Lord my Savior.   PSALM 38:21-22

WRITE Thy blessed name, O Lord, upon my heart, there to remain so indelibly engraven that no prosperity, no adversity shall ever move me from Thy love. Be Thou to me a strong Tower of defense, a Comforter in tribulation, a Deliverer in distress, a very present Help in trouble, and a Guide to heaven through the many temptations and dangers of this life. Amen.   THOMAS À KEMPIS

He went up into a mountain apart to pray: and when the evening was come, he was there alone.
                                    MATTHEW 14:23, KJV

But now, Lord, what do I look for? My hope is in you. Save me from all my transgressions; do not make me the scorn of fools.   PSALM 39:7-8

*I*F MY SOUL has turned perversely to
          the dark;
     If I have left some brother wounded by
          the way;
If I have preferred my aims to yours;
If I have been impatient and would not wait;
If I have marred the pattern drawn out for my
          life;
If I have cost tears to those I loved;
If my heart has murmured against your will,
     O Lord, forgive.   F. B. MEYER

I firmly believe a great many prayers are not answered because we are not willing to forgive someone.   DWIGHT L. MOODY

I waited patiently for the LORD; he turned to me and heard my cry. He lifted me out of the slimy pit, out of the mud and mire; he set my feet on a rock and gave me a firm place to stand.   PSALM 40:1-2

O GOD,
 In the crush of traffic, the push and
  shove of shopping, the surge in
corridors of school, we often wonder
 if we are known by you, or by anyone else.
In the isolation of apartments, the solitude of
 speeding automobiles, the seclusion of a
 nursing-home bed, we often wonder if we
 are remembered by you, or by anyone else.
Remind us anew, this day, O God, that you
 have the whole wide world in your hands.
Assure us, once more, that you know us, each
 one by name and by need.
Let us never feel forsaken, nor believe that
 multitudes are outside your providence.
Here and now, with fresh courage and full
 assurance, we call you Father, and
 together pray to you.   DAVID M. CURRIE

Prayer is exhaling the spirit of man and inhaling the spirit of God.   EDWIN KEITH

Do not withhold your mercy from me, O LORD; may
your love and your truth always protect me.

PSALM 40:11

O GOD, fill me with the knowledge of
your will through all spiritual wisdom
and understanding. I pray this in order
that I may live a life worthy of the Lord and may
please him in every way: bearing fruit in every
good work, growing in the knowledge of God,
being strengthened with all power according to
his glorious might. Then I may have great
endurance and patience, and joyfully give thanks
to the Father, who has qualified me to share in
the inheritance of the saints in the kingdom of
light. He has rescued me from the dominion of darkness and brought me into the kingdom of the Son
he loves, in whom I have redemption, the forgiveness of sins.   COLOSSIANS 1:9-12 (adapted)

God bless all those that I love; God bless all those
that love me; God bless all those that love those that
I love and all those that love those that love me.

A NEW ENGLAND SAMPLER

Blessed is he who has regard for the weak; the LORD delivers him in times of trouble. The LORD will protect him and preserve his life.   PSALM 41:1-2

O LORD, who wills that all your children should be one in you, I pray to you for the unity of your church. Pardon all our pride, and our lack of faith, of understanding and of charity, which are the cause of our divisions. Deliver us from our narrow-mindedness, from our bitterness, from our prejudices. Preserve us from considering as normal that which is a scandal to the world and an offense to your love. Teach us to recognize the gifts of thy grace among all those who call upon you.

THE LITURGY OF THE REFORMED
CHURCH OF FRANCE (adapted)

At church, with meek and unaffected grace,
His looks adorn'd the venerable place;
Truth from his lips prevail'd with double sway,
And fools, who came to scoff, remain'd to pray.

OLIVER GOLDSMITH

As the deer pants for streams of water, so my soul
pants for you, O God. My soul thirsts for God, for
the living God.   PSALM 42:1-2

O LORD
Here I am again
Just plain old me
Coming to You
As I've come a thousand times—
And this is what always happens:
Your response is immediate
You open Your arms unhesitatingly
You draw me to Yourself
You clasp me to Your Father-heart.
Then You reaffirm my position:
I am a child of the King
And all that is Yours is mine.
When I begin my stammering account
Of gross unworthiness
Your gentle smile hushes me.
With endless patience
You remind me once more
That my value never determines Your love.
Rather, Your love determines my value.

                                        RUTH HARMS CALKIN

One of his disciples said to him, "Lord, teach us to
pray."   LUKE 11:1, *NRSV*

Why are you downcast, O my soul? Why so disturbed within me? Put your hope in God, for I will yet praise him, my Savior and my God.   PSALM 43:5

ALMIGHTY GOD, I thank you because day after day has verified the truth of our Saviour's words: "Sufficient to the day is the evil thereof." Through the weakness and corruption of human nature and the unavoidable business of my station in life: in many unforeseen accidents and unexpected company: in cross occurrences, with abundance of other things incident to human life, I find occasion given to me daily to exercise virtues of one kind or another.

One day calls me to use justice and patience, and another prudence, temperance, and charity in forgiving injuries. I draw near unto you, the supreme fountain of virtue, for grace in the perplexed affairs of life, and thank you for every occasion on which I have found your strength to be made perfect in weakness; and I thank you that you are truth itself and that all your promises are yea and amen, through Jesus Christ, your mediator. Amen.   SUSANNA WESLEY

Pray, always pray; beneath sin's heaviest load, Prayer claims the blood from Jesus' side that flowed.

I do not trust in my bow, my sword does not bring me victory; but you give us victory over our enemies, you put our adversaries to shame.   PSALM 44:6-7

ALMIGHTY GOD, grant us grace to hear Jesus Christ, the heavenly bread, preached throughout the world and truly to understand him. May all evil, heretical and human doctrines be cut off, while your Word as the living bread be distributed. Amen.

MARTIN LUTHER

But you, dear friends, must build up your lives ever more strongly upon the foundation of our holy faith, learning to pray in the power and strength of the Holy Spirit.   JUDE 1:20, *TLB*

If we had forgotten the name of our God or spread out our hands to a foreign god, would not God have discovered it, since he knows the secrets of the heart?   PSALM 44:20-21

*O*UR FATHER, remove from us the sophistication of our age and the skepticism that has come, like frost, to blight our faith and to make it weak. We pray for a return of that simple faith, that old-fashioned trust in God, that made strong and great the homes of our ancestors who built this good land and who in building left us our heritage. In the strong name of Jesus, our Lord, we make this prayer. Amen.   PETER MARSHALL

Prayer has marked the trees across the wilderness of a skeptical world to direct the traveler in distress, and all paths lead to a single light.
                                          DOUGLAS MEADOR

Your throne, O God, will last for ever and ever; a
scepter of justice will be the scepter of your kingdom.
PSALM 45:6

O GOD, the God of all goodness and of all
grace, who art worthy of a greater love
than we can either give or understand:
Fill our hearts, we beseech you, with such love
toward you that nothing may seem too hard for
us to do or to suffer in obedience to your will;
and grant that thus loving you, we may become
daily more like unto you, and finally obtain the
crown of life which thou hast promised to those
that love you; through Jesus Christ our Lord.
BROOKE FOSS WESTCOTT

To be a branch means not only bearing fruit on
earth, but power in prayer to bring down blessing
from heaven. Abiding fully means praying much.
ANDREW MURRAY

God is our refuge and strength, an ever-present help
in trouble. Therefore we will not fear, though the
earth give way and the mountains fall into the
heart of the sea.   PSALM 46:1-2

GIVE ME open hands, O God, hands
ready to share with all who are in want
the blessings with which Thou hast
enriched my life. Deliver me from all meanness
and miserliness. Let me hold my money in
stewardship and all my worldly goods in trust
for Thee; to whom now be all honour and glory.
Amen.   JOHN BAILLIE

He prayeth well, who loveth well
Both man and bird and beast.
He prayeth best, who loveth best
All things both great and small;
For the dear God who loveth us,
He made and loveth all.

                          SAMUEL TAYLOR COLERIDGE

*Clap your hands, all you nations; shout to God
with cries of joy. How awesome is the LORD Most
High, the great King over all the earth!*

PSALM 47:1-2

O LORD JESUS, Let not your word
become a judgment upon us, that we
hear it and do it not, that we know it
and love it not, that we believe it and obey it not.
We ask this of you who lives eternally with the
Father and the Holy Spirit, world without end.
Amen.   THOMAS À KEMPIS

*Prayer is the incense of a holy heart
Rising to God from bruised and broken things,
When kindled by the Spirit's burning breath
And upward borne by faith's ascending wings.*

A. B. SIMPSON

Great is the LORD, and most worthy of praise, in the city of our God, his holy mountain.   PSALM 48:1

O LORD JESUS CHRIST, word and revelation of the eternal Father, come, we pray you, take possession of our hearts and reign where you have right to reign. So fill our minds with the thought and our imaginations with the picture of your love, that there may be in us no room for any desire that is discordant with your holy will. Cleanse us, we pray you, from all that may make us deaf to your call or slow to obey it, Who, with the Father and the Holy Spirit, art one God, blessed for ever.

WILLIAM TEMPLE

True prayer brings a person's will into accordance with God's will, not the other way around.

ANONYMOUS

But God will redeem my life from the grave; he will surely take me to himself.   PSALM 49:15

OSOVEREIGN and almighty Lord, bless all your people and all your flock. Give peace, your help, your love unto us, your servants, the sheep of your fold, that we may be united in the bond of peace and love, one body and one spirit, in one hope of our calling, in your divine and boundless love; for the sake of Jesus Christ, the great Shepherd of the sheep.

LITURGY OF SAINT MARK

I always love to begin a journey on Sundays, because I shall have the prayers of the church, to preserve all that travel by land, or by water.

JONATHAN SWIFT

Consider this, you who forget God, or I will tear you
to pieces, with none to rescue: He who sacrifices
thank offerings honors me, and he prepares the way
so that I may show him the salvation of God.

PSALM 50:22-23

MAKE ME to know your ways, O LORD;
teach me your paths.
Lead me in your truth, and teach me,
for you are the God of my salvation;
for you I wait all day long.

Be mindful of your mercy, O LORD, and of your
steadfast love,
for they have been from old.

Do not remember the sins of my youth or my
transgressions;
according to your steadfast love remember me,
for your goodness' sake, O LORD!

PSALM 25:4-7, NRSV

Trouble and perplexity drive me to prayer and
prayer drives away perplexity and trouble.

PHILIP MELANCHTHON

Have mercy on me, O God, according to your unfailing love; according to your great compassion blot out my transgressions. Wash away all my iniquity and cleanse me from my sin. PSALM 51:1-2

IN CONFIDENCE of Thy goodness and great mercy. O Lord, I draw near unto Thee, as a sick person to the Healer, as one hungry and thirsty to the Fountain of Life, a creature to the Creator, a desolate soul to my own tender Conforter. Behold, in Thee is all whatsoever I can or ought to desire. Rejoice therefore this day the soul of Thy servant; for unto Thee, O Lord, have I lifted up my soul. Amen.

THOMAS À KEMPIS

Plenteous grace with Thee is found,
Grace to cover all my sin;
Let the healing streams abound,
Make and keep me pure within. CHARLES WESLEY

*I trust in God's unfailing love for ever and ever. I
will praise you forever for what you have done; in
your name I will hope, for your name is good.*

PSALM 52:8-9

COME, my Light, and illumine my darkness.
Come, my Life and revive me from death.
Come, my Physician, and heal my wounds.
Come, Flame of divine love, and burn up the
thorns of my sins, kindling my heart
with the flame of your love.
Come, my King, sit upon the throne of my
heart and reign there.
For thou alone art my King and my Lord.

DIMITRI OF ROSTOV

*God answers sharp and sudden on some prayers,
And thrusts the thing we have
prayed for in our face,
A gauntlet with a gift in't.*

ELIZABETH BARRETT BROWNING

The fool says in his heart, "There is no God." They are corrupt, and their ways are vile; there is no one who does good.   PSALM 53:1

*L*ORD, why should I doubt any more, when you have given me such assured pledges of your love? First, you are my Creator, I your creature, you my Master, I your servant. But hence arises not my comfort: you are my Father, I your child. "You shall be my sons and daughters," says the Lord Almighty. Christ is my brother: "I ascend to my Father and your Father, to my God and your God"; but, lest this should not be enough, "your maker is your husband." Nay, more, I am a member of his body, he my head. Such privileges—had not the Word of truth made them known, who or where is the man that dared in his heart to have presumed to have thought it? So wonderful are these thoughts that my spirit fails in me at their consideration.

ANNE BRADSTREET

Spread out your petition before God, and then say, "Thy will, not mine, be done." The sweetest lesson I have learned in God's school is to let the Lord choose for me.   DWIGHT L. MOODY

Save me, O God, by your name; vindicate me by your might. Hear my prayer, O God; listen to the words of my mouth.   PSALM 54:1-2

O GOD ALMIGHTY, who made Heaven and earth and sea and all that is therein, help me, have mercy upon me, wash away my sins, save me in this world and in the world to come, through our Lord and Savior Jesus Christ, through whom is the glory and the power for ever and ever. Amen.

OXYRHYNCHUS PAPYRUS

Just when I need Him, He is my all,
Answering when upon Him I call;
Tenderly watching lest I should fall.

WILLIAM POOLE

But I call to God, and the LORD saves me. Evening, morning and noon I cry out in distress, and he hears my voice.   PSALM 55:16-17

O MY GOD, how does it happen in this poor old world that you are so great and yet nobody finds you, that you call so loudly and yet nobody hears you, that you are so near and yet nobody feels you, that you give yourself to everybody and yet nobody knows your name? Men flee from you and say they cannot find you; they turn their backs and say they cannot see you; they stop their ears and say they cannot hear you.   HANS DENCK

How those holy men of old could storm the battlements above! When there was no way to look but up, they lifted up their eyes to God who made the hills, with unshakeable confidence.

HERBERT LOCKYER

When I am afraid, I will trust in you. In God, whose word I praise, in God I trust; I will not be afraid. What can mortal man do to me?   PSALM 56:3-4

O LORD, who has mercy upon all, take away from me my sins, and mercifully kindle in me the fire of your Holy Spirit. Take away from me the heart of stone, and give me a heart of flesh, a heart to love and adore you, a heart to delight in you, to follow and to enjoy you, for Christ's sake.   AMBROSE

The fewer words, the better prayer.
MARTIN LUTHER

I will praise you, O Lord, among the nations; I will sing of you among the peoples. For great is your love, reaching to the heavens; your faithfulness reaches to the skies.   PSALM 57:9-10

O YOU who through the light of nature has aroused in us a longing for the light of grace, so that we may be raised in the light of your majesty, to you, I give thanks, Creator and Lord, that you allow me to rejoice in your works. Praise the Lord you heavenly harmonies, and you who know the revealed harmonies. For from him, through him and in him, all is, which is perceptible as well as spiritual; that which we know and that which we do not know, for there is still much to learn.

JOHANN KEPLER

Or what man is there among you who, if his son asks for bread, will give him a stone? Or if he asks for a fish, will he give him a serpent? If you then, being evil, know how to give good gifts to your children, how much more will your Father who is in heaven give good things to those who ask Him!

MATTHEW 7:9-11, *NKJV*

*The righteous will be glad when they are avenged.
. . . Then men will say, "Surely the righteous still
are rewarded; surely there is a God who judges the
earth."*   PSALM 58:10-11

*L*ORD, my heart is not large enough,
  my memory is not good enough,
  my will is not strong enough:
Take my heart and enlarge it,
Take my memory and give it quicker recall,
Take my will and make it strong
 and make me conscious of thee
   ever present,
   ever accompanying.   GEORGE APPLETON

*If your prayer is selfish, the answer will be
something that will rebuke your selfishness. You
may not recognize it as having come at all, but it is
sure to be there.*   WILLIAM TEMPLE

O my Strength, I watch for you; you, O God, are my
fortress, my loving God.   PSALM 59:9-10

I ARISE today
  Through a mighty strength:
    Christ to protect me today
  Against every poison,
  Against burning,
  Against drowning,
  Against deathly wounds,
  That I may receive abundant reward.

Christ with me, Christ before me,
Christ with me, Christ above,
Christ at my right, Christ at my left,
Christ in the fort, Christ in the chariot seat,
Christ on the poop deck,
Christ to every eye that sees me,
Christ in every ear that hears me,
That I may receive abundant reward.

I arise today through a mighty strength:
The strength of invocation of the Trinity.
Amen.   PATRICK OF IRELAND

Prayer is conversation with God.
                    CLEMENT OF ALEXANDRIA

You have shown your people desperate times; you have given us wine that makes us stagger. But for those who fear you, you have raised a banner to be unfurled against the bow.   PSALM 60:3-4

O GOD! I bless you for the wondrous revelation of yourself in Christ crucified, the wisdom of God, and the power of God. I bless you, that while man's wisdom leaves him helpless in presence of the power of sin and death, Christ crucified proves that he is the wisdom of God by the mighty redemption he works as the power of God. And I bless you, that what he wrought and bestows as an almighty Saviour is revealed within us by the divine light of your own Holy Spirit.   ANDREW MURRAY

For we know not what we should pray for as we ought: but the Spirit itself maketh intercession for us with groanings which cannot be uttered.
                                        ROMANS 8:26, KJV

Hear my cry, O God; listen to my prayer. From the ends of the earth I call to you, I call as my heart grows faint; lead me to the rock that is higher than I.

PSALM 61:1-2

O GOD
Help me to face myself honestly
In the revealing mirror of Your Word.
The longer I am a wife
The more utterly convinced I am
That there is only one solution
To personal discontent:
The complete surrender of myself
To Your method, Your schedule
Your Purpose, Your will.
If I am honestly willing to obey You
If I submit to Your Word
As my high standard
You will undertake the necessary surgery
To make me spiritually whole.
Surgery hurts, dear Lord—
No doubt about that.
But after the cutting comes healing
And You always send flowers!

RUTH HARMS CALKIN

Prayer is invading the impossible.

JACK W. HAYFORD

My soul finds rest in God alone; my salvation comes from him. He alone is my rock and my salvation; he is my fortress, I will never be shaken.
PSALM 62:1-2

I PRAY to you, the God of my Lord Jesus Christ, the Father of glory. Give to me a spirit of wisdom and revelation in the knowledge of him. Enlighten the eyes of my understanding that I may know what is the hope of his calling, what are the riches of his glorious inheritance in the saints, and what is the exceeding greatness of his power for me because I believe. You put this power to work in Christ when you raised him from the dead and seated him at your right hand in the heavenly places.
EPHESIANS 1:16-20 (adapted)

Prayer is communion with God, usually comprising petition, adoration, praise, confession, and thanksgiving.
INTERNATIONAL STANDARD BIBLE ENCYCLOPEDIA

*O God, you are my God, earnestly I seek you; my
soul thirsts for you, my body longs for you, in a dry
and weary land where there is no water.*

PSALM 63:1

LORD, make me an
instrument of your peace!
Where there is hatred,
let me show love;
where there is injury, pardon;
where there is doubt, faith;
where there is despair, hope;
where there is darkness, light;
and where there is sadness, joy.

FRANCIS OF ASSISI

*The prime need of the church is not men of money
nor men of brains, but men of prayer.*

E. M. BOUNDS

*Let the righteous rejoice in the LORD and take refuge
in him; let all the upright in heart praise him!*

PSALM 64:10

O GOD, I thank thee
for all the creatures thou hast made,
so perfect in their kind—
great animals like the elephant
    and the rhinoceros,
humorous animals like the camel
    and the monkey,
friendly ones like the dog and the cat,
working ones like the horse and the ox,
timid ones like the squirrel and the rabbit,
majestic ones like the lion and the tiger,
for birds with their songs.
O Lord, give us such love for thy creation,
that love may cast out fear,
and all thy creatures see in man
their priest and friend,
through Jesus Christ our Lord.

GEORGE APPLETON

*He offered a prayer so deeply devout that he seemed
kneeling and praying at the bottom of the sea.*

HERMAN MELVILLE, *Moby Dick*

*Blessed are those you choose and bring near to live
in your courts! We are filled with the good things of
your house, of your holy temple.*   PSALM 65:4

GRANT to us, O Lord, not to mind earthly
things, but rather to love heavenly
things, that whilst all things around us
pass away, we even now may hold fast to those
things which abide forever.   LEO THE GREAT

*Away in foreign fields they wondered how
    Their simple words had power—
At home the Christians, two or three, had met
    To pray an hour.
Yes, we are always wondering, wondering how—
    Because we do not see
Someone—perhaps unknown and far away—
    On bended knee.*   ANONYMOUS

*Shout with joy to God, all the earth! Sing the glory
of his name; make his praise glorious!*

PSALM 66:1-2

A LMIGHTY GOD, you have given us
grace at this time with one accord to
make our common supplication to you;
and you have promised through your well
beloved Son that when two or three are gathered
together in his name you will be in the midst of
them: Fulfill now, O Lord, our desires and
petitions as may be best for us; granting us in
this world knowledge of your truth and in the
age to come life everlasting. Amen.

JOHN CHRYSOSTOM

*O Lord, help me not to despise or oppose what I do
not understand.*   WILLIAM PENN

May God be gracious to us and bless us and make his face shine upon us, that your ways may be known on earth, your salvation among all nations.
                                                PSALM 67:1-2

I CONFESS, Lord, with thanksgiving, that you have made me in your image, so that I can remember you, think of you, and love you.

But that image is so worn and blotted out by faults, and darkened by the smoke of sin, that it cannot do that for which it was made, unless you renew and refashion it.

Lord, I am not trying to make my way to your height, for my understanding is in no way equal to that, but I do desire to understand a little of your truth which my heart already believes and loves.

I do not seek to understand so that I can believe, but I believe so that I may understand; and what is more, I believe that unless I do believe, I shall not understand.   ANSELM OF CANTERBURY

Prayer requires more of the heart than of the tongue.
                                                ADAM CLARKE

A father to the fatherless, a defender of widows, is God in his holy dwelling. God sets the lonely in families, he leads forth the prisoners with singing.

PSALM 68:5-6

FATHER, you are not only mine,
    but the Father of everyone who believes.
        By this I grasp, finally, why
    your Son taught us to say,
        "Our Father who is in heaven," not
        "My Father who is in heaven."

With freedom today I pray "our Father."
    These two words loose my loneliness
        and invade my isolation.
    They unlock the door of time
        and banish the barrier of space.

From the mountainside in Galilee
where he was asked, "Teach us to pray,"
    through countless lives until mine today
    a slender cord is stretching;
        braided and spliced with the faith
        of those who call you Father.

DANIEL PARTNER

Prayer is the spiritual gymnasium in which we exercise and practice godliness.   V. L. CRAWFORD

Praise be to the Lord, to God our Savior, who daily
bears our burdens. Our God is a God who saves;
from the Sovereign LORD comes escape from death.
                                          PSALM 68:19-20

I N ME there is darkness,
     But with you there is light;
     I am lonely, but you do not leave me;
I am feeble in heart, but with you there is help;
I am restless, but with you there is peace.
In me there is bitterness, but with you
               there is patience;
I do not understand your ways,
But you know the way for me.
                              DIETRICH BONHOEFFER

Teach me, O God, not to torture myself, not to make
a martyr out of myself through stifling reflection,
but rather teach me to breathe deeply in faith.
                              SÖREN KIERKEGAARD

*But I pray to you, O LORD, in the time of your favor;
in your great love, O God, answer me with your
sure salvation. Rescue me from the mire, do not let
me sink; deliver me from those who hate me, from
the deep waters.* PSALM 69:13-14

GOD, of your goodness, give me yourself
for you are sufficient for me. I cannot
properly ask anything less, to be
worthy of you. If I were to ask less, I should
always be in want. In you alone do I have all.

JULIAN OF NORWICH

*Sincerity is the prime requisite in every approach
to the God who requires "truth in the inward parts"
and who hates all hypocrisy, falsehood, and deceit.*

GEOFFREY B. WILSON

The poor will see and be glad—you who seek God, may your hearts live! The LORD hears the needy and does not despise his captive people.

PSALM 69:32-33

W E THANK YOU, Lord,
      That of your tender grace,
      In our distress
Thou hast not left us wholly comfortless.

We thank you, Lord,
That of your wondrous might,
Into our night
Thou hast sent down the glory of the Light.

We thank you, Lord,
That all your wondrous ways,
Through all your days,
Are wisdom, right, and ceaseless tenderness.

JOHN OXENHAM

Productive prayer requires earnestness, not eloquence.

ANONYMOUS

Yet I am poor and needy; come quickly to me, O God. You are my help and my deliverer; O LORD, do not delay.   PSALM 70:5

ALMIGHTY, ever-gracious Father, since all my salvation depends upon my having truly understood your holy Word, therefore grant that my heart be set free from worldly things so that I may with all diligence and faith hear and apprehend your holy Word. Do this that I may thereby understand your gracious will and in all sincerity live according to the same, to your praise and glory, through our Lord Jesus Christ. Amen.

JOHN CALVIN

Rejoice evermore. Pray without ceasing. In every thing give thanks: for this is the will of God in Christ Jesus concerning you.

1 THESSALONIANS 5:16-18, *KJV*

In you, O LORD, I have taken refuge; let me never be put to shame. Rescue me and deliver me in your righteousness; turn your ear to me and save me.

PSALM 71:1-2

GRACIOUS GOD, giving our neighbors
to us, and us to them,
and bidding us love our neighbors as
ourselves;
help us by loving to understand, and by
understanding to help,
and to have the grace to accept their help,
along the way to your Kingdom;
through Jesus Christ our Lord. Amen.

WILLIAM BOOTH

Not what we wish, but what we need,
   Oh! let your grace supply,
The good unasked, in mercy grant;
   The ill, though asked, deny.   JAMES MERRIK

Praise be to the LORD God, the God of Israel, who alone does marvelous deeds. Praise be to his glorious name forever; may the whole earth be filled with his glory. Amen and Amen.

PSALM 72:18-19

YOU TAKE the pen
and the lines dance.
You take the flute,
and the notes shimmer.
You take the brush, and the colors sing.
So all things have meaning and beauty in that
space beyond time where you are.
How, then, can I hold back anything from you?

DAG HAMMARSKJÖLD, God the Artist

To you, O Son of God, Lord Jesus Christ, as you pray to the eternal Father, we pray, make us one in him. Lighten our personal distress and that of our society. Receive us into the fellowship of those who believe. Turn our hearts, O Christ, to everlasting truth and healing harmony.

PHILIP MELANCHTHON

Those who are far from you will perish; you destroy all who are unfaithful to you. But as for me, it is good to be near God. I have made the Sovereign LORD my refuge.   PSALM 73:27-28

WE PRAY to Thee, O Christ, to keep us under the spell of immortality. May we never again think and act as if Thou wert dead. Let us more and more come to know Thee as a living Lord who hath promised to them that believe: "Because I live, ye shall live also."

Help us to remember that we are praying to the Conqueror of Death, that we may no longer be afraid nor be dismayed by the world's problems and threats, since Thou hast overcome the world. In Thy strong name, we ask for Thy living presence and Thy victorious power. Amen.

PETER MARSHALL

I have been driven many times to my knees by the overwhelming conviction that I had nowhere else to go.
ABRAHAM LINCOLN

But you, O God, are my king from of old; you bring salvation upon the earth. It was you who split open the sea by your power; you broke the heads of the monster in the waters.   PSALM 74:12-13

WHO is a God like you, pardoning iniquity
                and passing over the transgression
of the remnant of your possession?
You do not retain your anger forever because
                you delight in steadfast love.
You will again have compassion upon me; you
                will tread my iniquities under foot.
You will cast all my sins into the depths of
                the sea.   MICAH 7:18-19 (adapted)

Lord, if any have to die this day, let it be me, for I am ready.   BILLY BRAY

No one from the east or the west or from the desert can exalt a man. But it is God who judges: He brings one down, he exalts another.   PSALM 75:6-7

O LORD, the house of my soul is narrow; enlarge it that you may enter in. It is ruined, O repair it! It displeases your sight; I confess it, I know. But who shall cleanse it, or to whom shall I cry but unto you? Cleanse me from my secret faults, O Lord, and spare your servant from strange sins.   AUGUSTINE

Do I want to pray or only to think about my human problems? Do I want to pray or simply kneel there contemplating my sorrow? Do I want to direct my prayer towards God or let it direct itself towards me?
HUBERT VAN ZELLER

In Judah God is known; his name is great in Israel. . . . There he broke the flashing arrows, the shields and the swords, the weapons of war.

PSALM 76:1, 3

BLESSED LORD, through whose gift of the Holy Scriptures we learn of your mighty saving acts for mankind, help us so to hear, remember, and understand your Holy Word, that strengthened and sustained thereby, we may know in this temporal life the hope of eternity which you have given us in our Savior Jesus Christ, who lives and rules with you and the Holy Spirit now and ever. Amen.

DONALD J. SELBY

You art coming to a King,
Large petitions with you bring
For his grace and power are such
None can ever ask too much.   JOHN NEWTON

I cried out to God for help; I cried out to God to hear me. When I was in distress, I sought the Lord.

PSALM 77:1-2

WE UNDERSTAND, Father, that our temptations are common to man, and that You are faithful and will not suffer us to be tempted above what we are able to bear, but will with the temptation make a way to escape, so that we may be able to bear it. Help us to see the way of escape and take it. We pray for Your strength. Give us daily strength for daily needs.   JO PETTY

It is quite useless knocking at the door of heaven for earthly comfort. It's not the sort of comfort they supply there.   C. S. LEWIS

*We will tell the next generation the praiseworthy
deeds of the LORD, his power, and the wonders he
has done.*   PSALM 78:4

LORD GOD, you have placed me in your
church. You know how unsuitable I am.
Were it not for your guidance I would
long since have brought everything to destruc-
tion. I wish to give my heart and mouth to your
service. I desire to teach your people, and long
to be taught your work. Use me as your work-
man, dear Lord. Do not forsake me; for if I am
alone I shall bring all to nought. Amen.

MARTIN LUTHER

*We ought not to tolerate for a minute the ghastly
and grievous thought that God will not answer
prayer. History, as manifested in Christ Jesus,
demands it.*   CHARLES H. SPURGEON

Their hearts were not loyal to him, they were not faithful to his covenant. Yet he was merciful; he forgave their iniquities and did not destroy them.

PSALM 78:37-38

O LORD, prepare my heart, I beseech you, to reverence you, to adore you, to love you; to hate, for love of you, all my sins and imperfections, short-comings, whatever in me displeases you; and to love all which you love, and whom you love. Give me, Lord, fervour of love, shame for my unthankfulness, sorrow for my sins, longing for your grace, and to be wholly united with you. Let my very coldness call for the glow of your love; let my emptiness and dryness, like a barren and thirsty land, thirst for you, call on you to come into my soul, who refreshes those who are weary. Let my heart ache to you and for you, who stills the aching of the heart. Let my mute longings praise you, crave you, who satisfies the empty soul that waits on you.

E. B. PUSEY

Our ordinary views of prayer are not found in the New Testament. We look upon prayer as a means of getting things for ourselves; The Bible idea of prayer is that we may get to know God Himself.

OSWALD CHAMBERS

But they put God to the test and rebelled against the Most High; they did not keep his statutes. . . . When God heard them, he was very angry; he rejected Israel completely.   PSALM 78:56, 59

DEAR MASTER, in whose life I see
All that I would, but fail, to be,
Let your clear light forever shine,
To shame and guide this life of mine.

Though what I dream and what I do
In all my days are often two,
Help me, oppressed by things undone,
O you whose deeds and dreams were one.

JOHN HUNTER

Prayer serves as an edge and border to preserve the web of life from unraveling.   ROBERT HALL

He chose David his servant . . . to be the shepherd of his people Jacob, of Israel his inheritance. And David shepherded them with integrity of heart; with skillful hands he led them.   PSALM 78:70-72

O LORD, you have examined my heart and know everything about me. . . . You chart the path ahead of me, and tell me where to stop and rest. Every moment, you know where I am. You know what I am going to say before I even say it. . . .

This is too glorious, too wonderful to believe! I can *never* be lost to your Spirit! I can *never* get away from my God! If I go up to heaven, you are there; if I go down to the place of the dead, you are there. If I ride the morning winds to the farthest oceans, even there your hand will guide me, your strength will support me. . . .

Search me, O God, and know my heart; test my thoughts. Point out anything you find in me that makes you sad, and lead me along the path of everlasting life.   PSALM 139:1-10, 23-24, *TLB*

The deepest wishes of the heart find expression in secret prayer.   GEORGE E. REES

Help us, O God our Savior, for the glory of your name; deliver us and forgive our sins for your name's sake.   PSALM 79:9

*L*ORD JESUS CHRIST,
You were poor and in distress,
a captive and forsaken as I am.
You know all man's troubles;
You abide with me
when all men fail me;
You remember and seek me;
It is your will that I should know you
and turn to you.
Lord I hear your call and follow;
Help me.   DIETRICH BONHOEFFER

Trouble and prayer are closely related to each other. Prayer is of great value to trouble. Trouble often drives men to God in prayer, while prayer is but the voice of men in trouble.   E. M. BOUNDS

Restore us, O Lord God Almighty; make your face
shine upon us, that we may be saved.   PSALM 80:19

*L*ORD MY GOD, teach me, I beseech you,
to ask you aright for the right blessings.
Steer you the vessel of my life toward yourself, you tranquil haven of all storm-tossed
souls. Show me the course wherein I should go.
Renew a willing spirit within me. Let your Spirit
curb my wayward senses, and guide and enable
me unto that which is my true good, to keep
your laws, and in all my works evermore to
rejoice in your glorious and gladdening
presence. For yours is the glory and praise from
all your saints for ever and ever. Amen.

BASIL THE GREAT

Teach us to pray that we may cause
  The enemy to flee,
That we his evil power may bind,
  His prisoners to free.   WATCHMAN NEE

Sing for joy to God our strength; shout aloud to the God of Jacob! Begin the music, strike the tambourine, play the melodious harp and lyre.

PSALM 81:1-2

I THANK YOU for the house in which I live,
For the gray roof on which the raindrops
    slant;
I thank you for a garden and the slim
    young shoots
  That mark the old-fashioned things I plant.

I thank you for a daily task to do,
  For books that are my ships with golden
    wings.
For mighty gifts let others offer praise—
  Lord, I am thanking you for little things.

ANONYMOUS

Fear of trouble, present and future, often blinds us to the numerous small blessings we enjoy, silencing our prayers of praise and thanksgiving.

ANONYMOUS

God presides in the great assembly; he gives judgment among the "gods."   PSALM 82:1

ALMIGHTY GOD, I cannot possibly aspire vigorously toward you or have any clear perception of spiritual things without the assistance of your grace. Only the same almighty power that raised Jesus Christ from the dead can raise this soul of mine from the death of sin to a life of holiness. I do not question that power and I believe that these desires proceed from you. Give me faith and patience. Help me to wait for your enabling grace without discouragement, remembering the words of our Saviour, that men ought always to pray and not to faint. Amen.   SUSANNA WESLEY

Sometimes . . . God answers our prayers in the way our parents do, who reply to the pleas of their children with "Not just now" or "I'll have to think about that for a little while."   ROY M. PEARSON

Let them [your enemies] know that you, whose
name is the LORD—that you alone are the Most
High over all the earth.   PSALM 83:18

O GOD ALMIGHTY, who cleansed the
lips of the prophet Isaiah with a
burning coal: Cleanse my heart and my
lips: so grant to cleanse me, of your mercy, that
I may be able to proclaim worthily your holy
gospel: through Jesus Christ our Lord. Amen.

AMBROSE

O thou, by whom we come to God,
   The Life, the Truth, the Way,
The path of prayer Thyself hast trod—
   Lord teach us how to pray.

JAMES MONTGOMERY

How lovely is your dwelling place, O LORD Almighty! My soul yearns, even faints, for the courts of the LORD; my heart and my flesh cry out for the living God.   PSALM 84:1-2

GOD, why am I so often defeated?
Why am I so full of dread and anxiety?
Why am I so lamentably weak—
So perilously susceptible to temptation?
Why am I often inhospitable
So intolerant of the needs of others?
Why am I so undisciplined
So restless and dissatisfied?
Why do I protest so violently?
Above all, God
Why do I so frequently lose
The sense of Your shining Presence?
God, why?
Why?
Because you pray so little.   RUTH HARMS CALKIN

And this is the boldness we have in him, that if we ask anything according to his will, he hears us.
                          1 JOHN 5:14, *NRSV*

Will you not revive us again, that your people may rejoice in you? Show us your unfailing love, O LORD, and grant us your salvation.

PSALM 85:6-7

O GOD, sometimes I am tempted
because cheating seems to be the easiest
and quickest way to get what I want.
Forgive me for the times
I have told lies, kept miscounted change,
or misled my friends. Grant that I shall come to
love truth and hate lies—especially my own.
May all my words and deeds be free of sham
and make-believe.

In the classroom, in games
with my friends, as I trade at the store, help me
to be completely trustworthy.

Day by day may I live
in such close friendship with you that there
will be
nothing in my life
which is counterfeit or insincere. Amen.

WALTER L. COOK

You do not have because you do not ask.

JAMES 4:2, *NRSV*

Hear, O LORD, and answer me, for I am poor and needy. Guard my life, for I am devoted to you. You are my God; save your servant who trusts in you.

PSALM 86:1-2

OLORD GOD, ruler of the heaven and of the earth, creator of things visible and invisible, giver of eternal life, and consoler of the sorrowful, make me to stand firm in confession of your name that as with your aid I have begun the good fight, so with your aid I may be deemed worthy to gain the victory, lest the adversary spitefully mock at me saying: "Where is now her God in whom she trusted?"

But let the angel of your light come and restore to me the light which the darkness of my cell has taken from me; and let the right hand of your majesty scatter the phantom hosts of the ancient enemy. For we know, O Lord, that your mercy will aid us in all temptations.

MARGARET OF ANTIOCH

Ask and you will receive, so that your joy may be complete.   JOHN 16:24, NRSV

Indeed, of Zion it will be said, "This one and that one were born in her, and the Most High himself will establish her." The LORD will write a register of the peoples: "This one was born in Zion."

PSALM 87:5-6

DIVINE and gracious Savior, I ask You to take full possession of my heart and life. Let me know that each moment of today You are with me, protecting me with Your grace and preserving me through Your love. Help me to overcome the discouragements that are coming to me and ease my pain. Remove from my heart all self-pity, take all resentment from my mind, and let me live trustingly one day at a time as I lean on You. Give me a hopeful outlook for today, and remove all irritation from the coming night. Let my patience increase as I consider Your mercies, precious Savior. Amen.

MY PRAYER BOOK

In the war upon the powers of darkness, prayer is the primary and mightiest weapon, both in aggressive war upon them and their works; in the deliverance of men from their power; and against them as an hierarchy of powers opposed to Christ and His Church.   JESSIE PENN-LEWIS

O Lord, the God who saves me, day and night I cry out before you. May my prayer come before you; turn your ear to my cry.   PSALM 88:1-2

*O*LORD, our Heavenly Father, who orderest all things for our eternal good, mercifully enlighten our minds, and give us a firm and abiding trust in Thy love and care. Silence our murmurings, quiet our fears, and dispel our doubts, that rising above our afflictions and our anxieties, we may rest on Thee, the Rock of everlasting strength.

NEW CHURCH BOOK OF WORSHIP

Pray in the Spirit at all times in every prayer and supplication. To that end keep alert and always persevere.   EPHESIANS 6:18, *NRSV*

I will sing of the LORD's great love forever; with my mouth I will make your faithfulness known through all generations.   PSALM 89:1

LORD, you have taken the fear of death away from us. The end of our life here you have made the beginning of the true life. For a little while you will let our bodies rest in sleep, and then with the last trumpet you will wake them from their sleep.

You gave this earth of ours to keep for you, which you shaped with your own hands; and you will take it back again, and from a mortal, formless lump transform it into a thing of immortal beauty.

To free us from sin and from the curse laid upon us, you took both sin and the curse upon yourself.

If out of the weakness of human nature I have fallen and sinned in word or deed or thought, forgive it me; for you have power to forgive sins on earth. When I am divested of my body, may I stand before you with my soul unspotted: receive it, blameless and faultless, with your own hands.   MACRINA

Men ought always to pray, and not to faint.
                                    LUKE 18:1, *KJV*

Righteousness and justice are the foundation of
your throne; love and faithfulness go before you.
Blessed are those who have learned to acclaim you,
who walk in the light of your presence, O LORD.

PSALM 89:14-15

GOD, your name is Father.
The Son of your love
made known this name.
Please, keep me in its meaning.

Father, your name is Holy.
The people of today
don't know this name.
Please, show them its holiness.

Father, your children are holy.
The offspring of your life
who bear your name.
Please, hold them in its love.   DANIEL PARTNER

Prayer is the language of a man burdened with a
sense of need.   E. M. BOUNDS

How long, O LORD? Will you hide yourself forever? How long will your wrath burn like fire? Remember how fleeting is my life. For what futility you have created all men!   PSALM 89:46-47

I AM still not sure, God, what I want to do with my life. You see, I think there ought to be more to life than working. I'd like to have a family and spend some time with them. I want to be part of my children's lives while they're growing up. But I'm no slouch God. I work hard. I want to be good at what I do. But I want to be good at being a person first of all.

BILLINGS HODGETT

Work as if you were to live one hundred years; pray as if you were to die tomorrow.

BENJAMIN FRANKLIN

He who dwells in the shelter of the Most High will
rest in the shadow of the Almighty. I will say of the
LORD, "He is my refuge and my fortress, my God, in
whom I trust."   PSALM 91:1-2

I ARISE today
   Through a mighty strength,
   Strong virtue of invocation of the Trinity:
Through belief in the Threeness,
Through the confession of the Oneness
Of the Creator of creation.
I arise today
Through a mighty strength:
   The strength of the Incarnation of Christ,
   The strength of Christ in his Baptisms,
   The strength of his Crucifixion and his Burial,
   The strength of his Resurrection
         and his Ascension,
   The strength of his Coming on Judgment Day.
                                   PATRICK OF IRELAND

He who prays as he ought, will endeavor to live as
he prays.   JOHN OWEN

*It is good to praise the LORD and make music to
your name, O Most High, to proclaim your love in
the morning and your faithfulness at night.*

PSALM 92:1-2

*O*LORD, you are my God;
   I will exalt you, I will praise your name;
   for you have done wonderful things,
plans formed of old, faithful and sure. . . .
For you have been a refuge to the poor,
   a refuge to the needy in their distress,
   a shelter from the rainstorm and a shade
         from the heat.
When the blast of the ruthless was like a
         winter rainstorm,
   the noise of aliens like heat in a dry place,
you subdued the heat with the shade of clouds;
   the song of the ruthless was stilled.

ISAIAH 25:1, 4-5, *NRSV*

*Your Father knows what you need before you ask
him.*   MATTHEW 6:8, *NRSV*

Blessed is the man you discipline, O LORD, the man
you teach from your law; you grant him relief from
days of trouble, till a pit is dug for the wicked.

PSALM 94:12-13

HOLY LORD JESUS! Look upon your church, look upon our hearts. And wherever you see that there is not love like yours, oh, make haste and deliver your saints from all that is still selfish and unloving! Teach them to yield that self, which cannot love, to the accursed cross, to await the fate it deserves. Teach us to believe that we can love, because the Holy Spirit has been given us. Teach us to begin to love and serve, to sacrifice self and live for others, that love in action may learn its power, may be increased and perfected. Oh, teach us to believe that because you live in us, your love is in us too, and we can love as you do. Lord Jesus, you Love of God! your own Spirit is within us; oh, let him break through, and fill our whole life with love! Amen.   ANDREW MURRAY

Call to me and I will answer you, and will tell you
great and hidden things that you have not known.

JEREMIAH 33:3, NRSV

Come, let us bow down in worship, let us kneel before the LORD *our Maker; for he is our God and we are the people of his pasture, the flock under his care.*   PSALM 95:6-7

O LORD: Give to your people, we pray you, the spirit of truth and peace, that they may know you with all their minds; and that, following with all their hearts after those things which are pleasing to you, they ever may possess the gifts of your bountiful goodness.   LEO THE GREAT

Each of us is a person, with individual masks, scars, celebrations, moments of rejecting God, and experiences of conversion. Our prayers must spring from the indigenous soil of our own personal confrontation with the Spirit of God in our lives.
                                      MALCOLM BOYD

Sing to the LORD a new song, for he has done marvelous things; his right hand and his holy arm have worked salvation for him.   PSALM 98:1

TEACH US, good Lord, to serve You as You deserve; to give and not to count the cost; to fight and not to heed the wounds; to toil and not to ask for rest; to labour and not to ask for any reward save knowing that we do Your will. Through Jesus Christ our Lord.
                                    IGNATIUS OF LOYOLA

Heaven is never deaf but when man's heart is dumb.
                                    FRANCIS QUARLES

Exalt the LORD our God and worship at his holy mountain, for the LORD our God is holy.

PSALM 99:9

*L*OVING FATHER GOD, my heart is filled upon rethinking the greatness of your love and the completeness of your plan. I want to please you, but how often my flesh folds under the pressure of temptation.

I thank you that you know my frame, and you remember I am dust. And I thank you for the abundance of grace and the gift of your righteousness which you have made available to me through the cross of your Son.

Thank you for receiving me, gracious Lord. Amen.   JACK W. HAYFORD

When my children do wrong, I ache to hear their stumbling requests for forgiveness. I'm sure our heavenly Father aches even more deeply to hear from us.   AN UNKNOWN FATHER

For the LORD is good and his love endures forever;
his faithfulness continues through all generations.

PSALM 100:5

H ELP ME, O God, to be a good and a true
         friend,
         To be always loyal, and never to let
     my friends down;
Never to talk about them behind their backs
         in a way in which I would not do
         before their faces;
Never to betray a confidence or talk about the
         things about which I ought to be silent;
Always to be ready to share everything I have;
To be as true to my friends as I would wish
         them to be to me.
This I ask for the sake of him who is the
         greatest and truest of all friends. For
         Jesus' sake, amen.

WILLIAM BARCLAY

To pray together, in whatever tongue or ritual, is
the most tender brotherhood of hope and sympathy
that man can contract in this life.

ANNE GERMAINE DE STAËL

I will sing of your love and justice; to you, O LORD,
I will sing praise. I will be careful to lead a
blameless life—when will you come to me?

PSALM 101:1-2

ALMIGHTY GOD, in this hour of quiet I seek communion with Thee. From the fret and fever of the day's business, from the world's discordant noises, from the praise and blame of men, from the confused thoughts and vain imaginations of my own heart, I would now turn aside and seek the quietness of Thy presence. All day long have I toiled and striven; but now, in stillness of heart and in the clear light of Thine eternity, I would ponder the pattern my life has been weaving.   JOHN BAILLIE

O Lord, forgive what I have been, sanctify what I am, and order what I shall be.   ANONYMOUS

Hear my prayer, O LORD; let my cry for help come to you. Do not hide your face from me when I am in distress. Turn your ear to me; when I call, answer me quickly.   PSALM 102:1-2

GRANT US, O Lord, the blessing of those whose minds are stayed on you, so that we may be kept in perfect peace: a peace which cannot be broken. Let not our minds rest upon any creature, but only in the Creator; not upon goods, things, houses, lands, inventions of vanities or foolish fashions, lest, our peace being broken, we become cross and brittle and given over to envy. From all such deliver us, O God, and grant us your peace.

GEORGE FOX

No matter what may be the test,
   God will take care of you;
Lean weary one, upon His breast,
   God will take care of you.   C. D. MARTIN

Praise the LORD, O my soul; all my inmost being,
praise his holy name. Praise the LORD, O my soul,
and forget not all his benefits.   PSALM 103:1-2

Y OU ARE as faultless as the heaven is
      high, Almighty God.
      How can I comprehend you?
Your mind is fathomless.
How can I try to understand it?
I have this dilemma: Love inflames my heart
           and constrains me to speak.
Yet if I try to tell of your greatness,
           what shall I say?
How can I fathom your mysteries
           and your purposes?
How can I probe the limits of the Almighty?
You are far beyond comprehension for this
           finite mind of mine.
So it is with childlike simplicity that I try to
           worship and adore you,
and I merely whisper, *Father, with all my heart*
           I love you.   ROBERT C. SAVAGE

Prayer moves the hand that moves the world.
                              JOHN AIKMAN WALLACE

Praise the LORD, O my soul. O LORD my God, you are very great; you are clothed with splendor and majesty.   PSALM 104:1

COME and help us, Lord Jesus. A vision of your face will brighten us; but to feel your Spirit touching us will make us vigorous. Oh! for the leaping and walking of the man born lame. May we today dance with holy joy like David before the ark of God. May a holy exhilaration take possession of every part of us; may we be glad in the Lord; may our mouth be filled with laughter, and our tongue with singing, "for the Lord hath done great things for us whereof we are glad."   CHARLES H. SPURGEON

I don't know of a single foreign product that enters this country untaxed except the answer to prayer.
                                    MARK TWAIN

*How many are your works, O LORD! In wisdom you
made them all; the earth is full of your creatures.*

PSALM 104:24

L ORD GOD, heavenly Father, we know
that we are dear children of yours and
that you are our beloved Father, not
because we deserve it, nor ever could merit it,
but because our dear Lord, your only-begotten
Son, Jesus Christ, wills to be our brother, and of
his own accord offers and makes this blessing
known to us. Since we may consider ourselves
his brothers and sisters and he regards us as
such, you will permit us to become and remain
your children for ever. Amen.   MARTIN LUTHER

*Prayer is a rising up and a drawing near to God in
mind and in heart, and in spirit.*

ALEXANDER WHYTE

Look to the LORD and his strength; seek his face always. Remember the wonders he has done, his miracles, and the judgments he pronounced.

PSALM 105:4-5

*L*ORD, make me aware of . . .
Sunlight filtering through the trees
The song of the March wind
Crickets at twilight
Water splashing in soapsuds
Yellow daffodils in a crystal vase
Delicate china on pink mats
The aroma of fresh coffee
The first day of spring
Green peas and red beets
A dewdrop on a rose
Freckles on a grinning face
The longing in my husband's eyes.

RUTH HARMS CALKIN

Prayer is the golden key that opens heaven.

THOMAS WATSON

He sent a man before them—Joseph, sold as a slave.
They bruised his feet with shackles, his neck was
put in irons, till what he foretold came to pass, till
the word of the LORD proved him true.

PSALM 105:17-19

O LORD our God, refresh me with quiet sleep, when I am wearied with the day's labor; that being assisted with the help which my weakness needs, I may be devoted to you both in body and mind; through Jesus Christ our Lord.

Be present, O Lord, to my prayers, and protect me by day and night that in all successive changes of times I may ever be strengthened by your unchangeableness; through Jesus Christ our Lord.

THE LEONINE SACRAMENTARY (adapted)

Every chain that spirits wear
Crumbles in the breath of prayer.

JOHN GREENLEAF WHITTIER

He [the LORD] brought out Israel, laden with silver and gold, and from among their tribes no one faltered.   PSALM 105:37

O GOD, whose eternal providence has embarked our soul in our bodies, not to expect any port of anchorage on the sea of this world, to steer directly through it to your glorious kingdom, preserve us from the dangers that on all sides assault us, and keep our affections still fitly disposed to receive your holy inspirations, that being carried strongly forward by your Holy Spirit we may happily arrive at last in the haven of eternal salvation, through our Lord Jesus Christ.   JOHN WESLEY

Now I am past all comforts here, but prayers.
                          WILLIAM SHAKESPEARE, *Henry VIII*

Praise the LORD. Give thanks to the LORD, for he is good; his love endures forever.   PSALM 106:1

O LORD JESUS CHRIST, who embraces children with the arms of your mercy, and makes them living members of your Church; give them grace, we pray, to stand fast in your faith, to obey your word, and to abide in your love; that, being made strong by your Holy Spirit, they may resist temptation and overcome evil, and may rejoice in the life that now is, and dwell with you in the life that is to come; through your merits, O merciful Saviour, who with the Father and Holy Ghost lives and reigns one God, world without end. Amen.

THE BOOK OF COMMON PRAYER

In the midst of the plots, execution, and arrest of Peter, Luke injects the very important word, "but." Herod's plan was to execute him, but the believers were praying for Peter's safety.

LIFE APPLICATION BIBLE on Acts 12:5

They [the Israelites] forgot the God who saved them, who had done great things in Egypt. . . . So he said he would destroy them.   PSALM 106:21, 23

*L*ORD JESUS, we come to Thee now as little children. Dress us again in clean pinafores; make us tidy once more with the tidiness of true remorse and confession. O, wash our hearts, that they may be clean again.

Make us to know the strengthening joys of the Spirit, and the newness of life which only Thou canst give. Amen.   PETER MARSHALL

Pray, always pray; when sickness wastes thy
     frame,
Prayer brings the healing power of Jesus' name.
                                        A. B. SIMPSON

*Save us, O LORD our God, and gather us from the
nations, that we may give thanks to your holy name
and glory in your praise.*   PSALM 106:47

*H*ELP ME, O Lord, to make a true use of
all disappointments and calamities in
this life, in such a way that they may
unite my heart more closely with you. Cause
them to separate my affections from worldly
things and inspire my soul with more vigor in
the pursuit of true happiness. SUSANNA WESLEY

*Whenever you pray, go into your room and shut the
door and pray to your Father who is in secret; and
your Father who sees in secret will reward you.*
                              MATTHEW 6:6, NRSV

Give thanks to the LORD, *for he is good; his love endures forever.*   PSALM 107:1

FROM ALL ETERNITY, O Jesus Christ, you have been our Lord and our God: so did the Father will it. Yet in this, the last of all periods of time, you also had your birth; you were born of a virgin, of one that had no knowledge of any man. To redeem us from the Law, you submitted to the Law. Your purpose was to free us from the slavery to which our corruption had reduced us and to confer upon us the rank of sons.

Deliver us, now, Lord, from all that is vain; fulfill your promise and free us from sin and shame; fill our hearts with your Holy Spirit and enable us to say: "Abba, Father."

A SYRIAC LITURGY (adapted)

They who have steeped their soul in prayer
  Can every anguish calmly bear.

RICHARD M. MILNES

Be exalted, O God, above the heavens, and let your glory be over all the earth. Save us and help us with your right hand, that those you love may be delivered.   PSALM 108:5-6

O GOD, we have known and believed the love which Thou hast for us. May we, by dwelling in love, dwell in Thee and Thou in us. May we learn to love Thee Whom we have not seen, by loving our brethern whom we have seen. Teach us, O heavenly Father, the love wherewith Thou hast loved us; fashion us, O blessed Lord, after Thine own example of love; shed abroad, O Thou Holy Spirit of Love, the love of God and man in our hearts. Amen.

HENRY ALFORD

Pray till you pray.   D.M. MCINTYRE

But you, O Sovereign LORD, deal well with me for your name's sake; out of the goodness of your love, deliver me. For I am poor and needy, and my heart is wounded within me.   PSALM 109:21-22

O CHRIST, who camest not to be ministered unto but to minister, have mercy upon all who labour faithfully to serve the common good. O Christ, who didst feed the hungry multitude with loaves and fishes, have mercy upon all who labour to earn their daily bread. O Christ, who didst call unto Thyself all them that labour and are heavy laden, have mercy upon all whose work is beyond their strength. And to Thee, with the Father and the Holy Spirit, be all the glory and the praise. Amen.

JOHN BAILLIE

For everything God made is good, and we may eat it gladly if we are thankful for it, and if we ask God to bless it, for it is made good by the Word of God and prayer.   1 TIMOTHY 4:4-5, TLB

The LORD says to my Lord: "Sit at my right hand until I make your enemies a footstool for your feet."
PSALM 110:1

GRACIOUS GOD, Heavenly Father, I must confess that I am sometimes upset by the many changes that come in life. I find it difficult to make the necessary adjustments. I do not ask to understand, but help me, I pray You, always to realize that no matter what happens to me, and what changes must me made, You still love me and will make every experience work together for my good.

Give me the faith to trust Your promise, "My grace is sufficient for you." In mercy forgive all grumbling and complaining of which I have been guilty in the past. Teach me to follow the example of Jesus, my Savior and Lord, who in trial and tribulation said, "Not My will, but Thine, be done." In that spirit I shall be able to meet whatever life has in store for me. For Jesus' sake, amen.   *MY PRAYER BOOK*

By prayer, the ability is secured to feel the law of love, to speak according to the law of love, and to do everything in harmony with the law of love.
E. M. BOUNDS

Praise the LORD. *I will extol the* LORD *with all my heart in the council of the upright and in the assembly.*   PSALM 111:1

FILL THOU my life, O Lord my God,
   In ev'ry part with praise,
   That my whole being may proclaim
Thy being and Thy ways.
Not for the lip of praise alone,
   Nor e'en the praising heart,
I ask, but for a life made up
   Of praise in every part:
Praise in the common things of life,
   Its goings out and in;
Praise in each duty and each deed,
   However small and mean.
Fill every part of me with praise;
   Let all my being speak
Of Thee and of Thy love,
   O Lord, Poor though I be and weak.
So shall no part of day nor night
   From sacredness be free,
But all my life, in every step,
         Be fellowship with Thee.
                    HORATIUS BONAR

God receives little thanks, even for his greatest gifts.   ANONYMOUS

Praise the LORD. Blessed is the man who fears the LORD, who finds great delight in his commands.

PSALM 112:1

THERE is one thing I ask of the LORD, the thing I seek most of all: to live in the house of the LORD all the days of my life, to behold the beauty of the LORD, and to inquire in his temple.

For he will hide me in his shelter in the day of trouble; he will conceal me under the cover of his tent; he will set me high on a rock.

Now my head is lifted up above my enemies, and I will offer in his tent sacrifices with shouts of joy; I will sing and make melody to the LORD.

PSALM 27:4-6 (adapted)

Without the incense of heartfelt prayer, even the greatest of cathedrals is dead.   ANONYMOUS

Who is like the LORD our God, the One who sits enthroned on high, who stoops down to look on the heavens and the earth? He raises the poor from the dust and lifts the needy from the ash heap.

PSALM 113:5-7

*L*ORD, who has mercy upon all, take away from me my sins, and mercifully kindle in me the fire of your Holy Spirit. Take away from me the heart of stone, and give me a heart of flesh, a heart to love and adore you, a heart to delight in you, to follow and to enjoy you. For Christ's sake, amen.   AMBROSE

And whenever you pray, do not be like the hypocrites; for they love to stand and pray in the synagogues and at the street corners, so that they may be seen by others.   MATTHEW 6:5, NRSV

Not to us, O LORD, not to us but to your name be the glory, because of your love and faithfulness.

PSALM 115:1

BLESSED LORD! I see why my prayer has not been more believing and prevailing. I was more occupied with my speaking to you than your speaking to me. I did not understand that the secret of faith is this: there can be only so much faith as there is of the Living Word dwelling in the soul.

And your Word had taught me so clearly: Let every man be swift to hear, slow to speak; let not your heart be hasty to utter anything before God.

Lord, teach me that it is only with your Word taken up into my life that my words can be taken into your heart; that your work, if it is a living power within me, will be a living power with you; what your mouth has spoken your hand will perform.   ANDREW MURRAY

Do not have as your motive the desire to be known as a praying man. Get an inner chamber in which to pray where no one knows you are praying, shut the door, and talk to God in secret.

OSWALD CHAMBERS

*I love the L*ORD*, for he heard my voice; he heard my cry for mercy. Because he turned his ear to me, I will call on him as long as I live.*   PSALM 116:1-2

O ETERNAL and most glorious God . . . You who assure us that precious in your sight is the death of your saints, enable us in life and death, seriously to consider the value, the price of a soul. It is precious, O Lord, because your image is stamped and imprinted upon it; precious, because the blood of your Son was paid for it; precious, because your blessed Spirit, the Holy Ghost works upon it, and tests it, by his various fires; and precious, because it is entered into your revenue and made a part of your treasure.   JOHN DONNE

The wings of prayer carry high and far.
                                    ANONYMOUS

Praise the LORD, all you nations; extol him, all you peoples. For great is his love toward us.

PSALM 117:1-2

J ESUS, my own kind of love is flawed and conditional. I think I'd like to love the way you do—but I know you'll have to give it to me because I can't manufacture it. Please fill me with your Spirit, and soften my heart toward others. When someone treats me badly, whisper to me again, "Father forgive them, for they know not what they do."   PAT BOONE

Our prayers must mean something to us if they are to mean anything to God.   MALTBIE D. BABCOCK

*Give thanks to the LORD, for he is good; his love
endures forever.*   PSALM 118:1

I ARISE today
   Through a mighty strength:
      God's power to guide me,
   God's might to uphold me,
   God's wisdom to teach me,
   God's eyes to watch over me,
   God's ear to hear me,
   God's Word to give me speech,
   God's hand to guard me,
   God's way to lie before me,
   God's shield to shelter me,
   God's host to secure me:
      Against the snares of devils,
      Against the seductions of vices,
      Against the lusts of nature,
      Against everyone who shall wish me ill,
      Whether far or near, many or few.

                              PATRICK OF IRELAND

*A person must recognize his need for God before he
can request divine aid and give God due thanks.*

                              ANONYMOUS

You are my God, and I will give you thanks; you are my God, and I will exalt you. Give thanks to the LORD, for he is good; his love endures forever.

PSALM 118:28-29

O JESUS CHRIST, the mirror of all gentleness of mind, the example of highest obedience and patience, grant me your servant true devotion to consider how you, innocent and undefiled Lamb, were bound, taken, and hauled away to death for my sins; how well content you were to suffer such things, not opening your mouth in impatience, but willingly offering yourself unto death. O gracious God, how vilely were you mishandled for my sake! O Lord, let this never come out of my heart. Expel through its coldness and sloth, stir up love and fervency towards you; provoke me to earnest prayer and make me cheerful and diligent in your will. Amen.   MILES COVERDALE (adapted)

He went forward a little, and fell face downward on the ground, and prayed.   MATTHEW 26:39, *TLB*

Blessed are they whose ways are blameless, who
walk according to the law of the LORD.

PSALM 119:1

YOUR THRONE, O God, is forever and
ever, and the righteous scepter is the
scepter of your kingdom. You have
loved righteousness and hated wickedness;
therefore God, even your God, has anointed you
with the oil of gladness beyond your com-
panions.

In the beginning, Lord, you founded the
earth, and the heavens are the work of your
hands; they will perish, but you remain; they
will all wear out like clothing; like a cloak you
will roll them up, and like clothing they will be
changed. But you are the same, and your years
will never end.   HEBREWS 1:8-12 (adapted)

The efficacy of prayer is founded on the depend-
ability of God.   ANONYMOUS

Do good to your servant, and I will live; I will obey your word. Open my eyes that I may see wonderful things in your law.   PSALM 119:17-18

O LORD GOD, in whom we live, and move, and have our being, open our eyes that we may behold your fatherly presence ever about us. Draw our hearts to you with the power of your love. Teach us to be careful for nothing, and when we have done what you have given us to do, help us, O God, our Saviour, to leave the issue to your wisdom. Take from us all doubt and distrust. Lift our thoughts up to thee in heaven, and make us to know that all things are possible to us through thy Son, our Redeemer.   BROOKE FOSS WESTCOTT

Lord, take my lips and speak through them; take my mind and think through it; take my heart and set it on fire.   W. H. H. AITKEN

Teach me, O LORD, to follow your decrees; then I will keep them to the end. Give me understanding, and I will keep your law and obey it with all my heart.   PSALM 119:33-34

*L*ORD JESUS, I know you have clearly shown us the pattern for prayer. But it seems you put the hard part first: The Father's name, his kingdom, and his will. I am eloquent when praying for daily bread, forgiveness, or deliverance. Yet, I have few holy words when I consider the holiness of my Father's name. Also, how can I truthfully pray for the kingdom's coming? I am so little ruled by the King. And, can a rebel pray for another's will?

O Lord! I want what the Father can daily provide but often don't live as a child of a heavenly Father. I seek his forgiveness but don't live in the love that forgives. I tend toward temptation and don't cry for rescue.

Oh, my life prevents my prayer! So I gather with your disciples again and with them ask once more, "Lord, teach us to pray."

DANIEL PARTNER

Do not pray by heart but with the heart.

ANONYMOUS

You are my portion, O LORD; I have promised to obey your words. I have sought your face with all my heart; be gracious to me according to your promise.   PSALM 119:57-58

GRANT ME, O most merciful Jesus, your grace, that it may be with me, and labour with me, and abide with me even to the end.

Give me grace ever to desire and to will what is most acceptable to you and most pleasing in your sight.

Let your will be mine, and let my will ever follow yours, and fully accord with it.

Let there be between you and me but one will, so that I may love what you love, and abhor what you hate; and let me not be able to will any thing which you do not will, nor to dislike any thing which you do will.   THOMAS À KEMPIS

Prayer is the spirit speaking truth to Truth.
                                    PHILIP JAMES BAILEY

I know, O LORD, that your laws are righteous, and in faithfulness you have afflicted me. May your unfailing love be my comfort, according to your promise to your servant.   PSALM 119:75-76

*O*HEAVENLY FATHER, your hand replenishes all living creatures with blessing and gives meat to the hungry in due season; I acknowledge my meat and drink to be your gifts, prepared by your fatherly providence to be received by me for the comfort of my body with thanksgiving: I most humbly beg you to bless me and my food and to give me grace so to use these your benefits that I may be thankful to you and liberal to my poor neighbors, through Jesus Christ our Lord. Amen.

THOMAS BECON (adapted)

Do I want to pray or only to think about my human problems? Do I want to pray or simply kneel there contemplating my sorrow? Do I want to direct my prayer towards God or let it direct itself towards me?

HUBERT VAN ZELLER

My soul faints with longing for your salvation, but I have put my hope in your word.   PSALM 119:81

I WANT to be teachable, Lord. Is there something You want to show me, some block You want removed, some change You want in me or my attitudes before You can answer my prayer? Give me the gift of eyes that see, of ears that hear what You are saying to me.

Come Lord Jesus, and abide in my heart. How grateful I am to realize that the answer to my prayer does not depend on me at all. As I quietly abide in You and let Your life flow into me, what freedom it is to know that the Father does not see my threadbare patience or insufficient trust, rather only Your patience, Lord, and Your confidence that the Father has everything in hand.

In Your faith I thank You right now for a more glorious answer to my prayer than I can imagine. Amen.   CATHERINE MARSHALL

Father, forgive us our trash baskets, as we forgive those who put their trash in our baskets.
                                        A YOUNG CHILD

Oh, how I love your law! I meditate on it all day long. Your commands make me wiser than my enemies, for they are ever with me.

PSALM 119:97-98

GRANT, ALMIGHTY GOD, that as you have, in various ways, testified and daily also prove how dear and precious to you is humanity as we enjoy daily so many and so remarkable proofs of your goodness and favor— O grant that we learn to rely wholly on your goodness. You have brought endless examples of your goodness before us, which you would have us continually to experience, that we may not only pass through our earthly course, but also confidently aspire to the hope of that blessed and celestial life which is laid up for us in heaven; through Christ alone, our Lord. Amen.

JOHN CALVIN

Prayer is essentially man standing before his God in wonder, awe, and humility; man, made in the image of God, responding to his maker.

GEORGE APPLETON

Sustain me according to your promise, and I will live; do not let my hopes be dashed. Uphold me, and I will be delivered; I will always have regard for your decrees.   PSALM 119:116-117

GIVE US GRACE, O Lord, to work while it is day, fulfilling diligently and patiently whatever duty Thou appointest us; doing small things in the day of small things, and great labors if Thou summon us to any. . . .Go with me, and I will go; but if Thou go not with me, send me not; let me hear Thy voice when I follow. Amen.   CHRISTINA ROSSETTI

You need not cry very loud; he is nearer to us than we think.   BROTHER LAWRENCE

Your statutes are wonderful; therefore I obey them.
The unfolding of your words gives light; it gives
understanding to the simple.   PSALM 119:129-130

O LORD, I give myself to Thee, I trust
Thee wholly. Thou art wiser than I—
more loving to me than I myself. Deign
to fulfill Thy high purposes in me whatever they
be—work in and through me. I am born to serve
Thee, to be Thine, to be Thy instrument. Let me
be Thy blind instrument. I ask not to see—I ask
not to know—I ask simply to be used.

JOHN HENRY NEWMAN

Prayer does not change God, but it changes him
who prays.   SÖREN KIERKEGAARD

Your compassion is great, O LORD; preserve my life according to your laws. Many are the foes who persecute me, but I have not turned from your statutes.   PSALM 119:156-157

LORD JESUS, I ask with Peter of old: How often must I forgive those who sin against me and offend me? O Lord, if I am to forgive seventy times seven, then You must give me the grace and the will to do so. My sinful heart is resentful and often filled with bitterness against others. So often I have been hurt and sinned against. I must confess to You, Lord Jesus, that I do not find it easy to forgive and forget. Help me, O Lord.

I know You have forgiven me times without number. That is why I am coming to You, asking for help. Enable me in all sincerity of heart to say as You did on the cross: Father, forgive them; and then help me to forgive as You have forgiven me more than seventy times seven.

Hear my plea, gracious Lord. Amen.

MY PRAYER BOOK

Pray not for lighter burdens but for stronger backs.
                                        THEODORE ROOSEVELT

I call on the LORD in my distress, and he answers me. Save me, O LORD, from lying lips and from deceitful tongues.   PSALM 120:1-2

SAVE ME, O God! For the waters have come up to my neck. I sink in deep mire, where there is no foothold; I have come into deep waters, and the flood sweeps over me. I am weary with my crying; my throat is parched. My eyes grow dim with waiting for my God.

O God, You know my folly; the wrongs I have done are not hidden from You. But as for me, my prayer is to You, O Lord. At an acceptable time, O God, in the abundance of Your steadfast love, answer me.

Answer me, O Lord, for Your steadfast love is good; according to Your abundant mercy, turn to me. Hide not Your face from Your servant; for I am in distress—hurry to answer me. Draw near to me, redeem me. Amen.   PSALM 69 (adapted)

I would have no desire other than to accomplish thy will. Teach me to pray; pray thyself in me.

FRANCIS FENELON

I lift up my eyes to the hills—where does my help come from? My help comes from the LORD, the Maker of heaven and earth.   PSALM 121:1-2

I THANK YOU, O God, for the relief and satisfaction of mind that come with the firm assurance that you govern the world; for the patience and resignation to your providence that are afforded as I reflect that even the tumultuous and irregular actions of the sinful are, nevertheless, under your direction, who are wise, good, and omnipotent, and have promised to make all things work together for good to those who love you.   SUSANNA WESLEY

Ask, and it will be given you; search, and you will find; knock, and the door will be opened.
                                             MATTHEW 7:7, NRSV

I rejoiced with those who said to me, "Let us go to the house of the LORD." Our feet are standing in your gates, O Jerusalem. PSALM 122:1-2

O H, I LONG to be filled more with God! Lord, stir me up more in earnest. I want to be more like Jesus. I see that nothing will do but being continually filled with the divine presence and glory. I know all that you have is mine, but I want to feel a close union. Lord, increase my faith. WILLIAM CARVOSSO

Oh, what a cause of thankfulness it is that we have a gracious God to go to on all occasions! Use and enjoy this privilege and you can never be miserable. Oh, what an unspeakable privilege is prayer!
LADY MAXWELL

As the eyes of slaves look to the hand of their master, as the eyes of a maid look to the hand of her mistress, so our eyes look to the LORD our God, till he shows us his mercy.   PSALM 123:2

FOR OUR ABSENT loved ones we implore your loving-kindness. Keep them in life, keep them in glowing honor; and for us, grant that we remain worthy of their love. For Christ's sake, let not our beloved blush for us, nor we for them. Grant us but that, and grant us courage to endure lesser ills unshaken, and to accept death, loss, and disappointment as it were straws upon the tide of life.

ROBERT LOUIS STEVENSON

Epaphras . . . greets you. He is always wrestling in his prayers on your behalf. COLOSSIANS 4:12, *NRSV*

Praise be to the LORD, who has not let us be torn by their teeth. We have escaped like a bird out of the fowler's snare; the snare has been broken, and we have escaped.   PSALM 124:6-7

WHEN THE SIGNS of age begin to mark my body (and still more when they touch my mind); when the ill that is to diminish me or carry me off strikes from without or is born within me; when the painful moment comes in which I suddenly awaken to the fact that I am ill or growing old; and above all at that last moment when I feel I am losing hold of myself and am absolutely passive within the hands of the great unknown forces that have formed me; in all those dark moments, O God, grant that I may understand that it is you (provided only my faith is strong enough) who are painfully parting the fibers of my being in order to penetrate to the very marrow of my substance and bear me away within yourself.

TEILHARD DE CHARDIN

Devote yourselves to prayer, keeping alert in it with thanksgiving.   COLOSSIANS 4:2, *NRSV*

Those who trust in the LORD are like Mount Zion,
which cannot be shaken but endures forever.

PSALM 125:1

*O*H, THE DEPTHS of the riches both of
your wisdom and knowledge, O God!
How unsearchable are your judgments
and your ways are past finding out.
Your greatness cannot be imagined.
You are greater than all language, and no
words can express your majesty.
You are above all, outside of all, and beyond
all I can even imagine.
You are without limit.
When I speak of you I cannot refer to amount
or size or weight, for you are beyond
measure.
You are not less or more, large or small.
You are simply God, the infinite One.
A human mind has no capacity to comprehend you.
What I can do is praise, adore, and worship you.

ROBERT C. SAVAGE

God deserves far more praise than any of us could
ever give Him.   ANONYMOUS

The LORD has done great things for us, and we are filled with joy. Restore our fortunes, O LORD, like streams in the Negev.   PSALM 126:3-4

ALMIGHTY GOD, give me a measure of true religion and thereby set me free from vain and disappointing hopes, from lawless and exorbitant appetites, from frothy and empty joys, from anxious, self-devouring cares, from a dull and black melancholy, from an eating envy and swelling pride, and from rigid sourness and severity of spirit, so that I may possess that peace which passes all understanding, through Jesus Christ our Lord.

BENJAMIN WHICHCOTE (adapted)

God give me work
Till my life shall end
And life
Till my work is done.

EPITAPH, WINIFRED HOLTBY

Unless the LORD builds the house, its builders labor in vain. Unless the LORD watches over the city, the watchmen stand guard in vain.   PSALM 127:1

*O*GOD our Father, Good beyond all that is good, Fair beyond all that is fair, in whom is calmness and peace: do thou make up the dissensions which divide us from each other, and bring us back into an unity of love, which may bear some likeness to Thine divine nature. Grant us that we may be spiritually one, as well in ourselves as in each other, through that peace of Thine which maketh all things peaceful, and through the grace, mercy, and tenderness of Thine only Son. Amen.

JACOBITE LITURGY OF SAINT DIONYSIUS

Seven days without prayer makes one weak.
ALLEN E. BARTLETT

Blessed are all who fear the LORD, *who walk in his ways. You will eat the fruit of your labor; blessings and prosperity will be yours.*   PSALM 128:1-2

O GOD ALMIGHTY, Father of our Lord Jesus Christ, grant us, we pray you, to be grounded and settled in your truth by the coming down of the Holy Spirit into our hearts. That which we know not, do reveal; that which is wanting in us, do fill up; that which we know, do confirm, and keep us blameless in your service, through the same Jesus Christ our Lord.

CLEMENT OF ROME

O Jesus, Son of God, who was silent before Pilate, do not let us wag our tongues without thinking of what we are to say and how to say it.

GAELIC PRAYER

Plowmen have plowed my back and made their furrows long. But the LORD is righteous; he has cut me free from the cords of the wicked.

PSALM 129:3-4

I ASKED for strength that I might achieve;
    I was made weak that I might learn
        humbly to obey.
I asked for health that I might do greater things;
    I was given infirmity that I might do better things.
I asked for riches that I might be happy;
    I was given poverty that I might be wise.
I asked for power that I might have the praise of men;
    I was given weakness that I might feel the
        need of God.
I asked for all things that I might enjoy life;
    I was given life that I might enjoy all things.
I got nothing that I had asked for,
    but everything that I had hoped for.
Almost despite myself my unspoken prayers
        were answered;
    I am, among all men, most richly blessed.

AN UNKNOWN CONFEDERATE SOLDIER

Our prayers are often filled with selfish "wants"; God always answers with what we need.

ANONYMOUS

I wait for the LORD, *my soul waits, and in his word
I put my hope. My soul waits for the Lord more than
watchmen wait for the morning.*   PSALM 130:5-6

O LORD,
    let nothing divert my advance towards
        you,
but in this dangerous labyrinth of the world
        and the whole course of my
        pilgrimage here,
May your heavenly dictates be my map and
        your holy life be my guide.

                          JOHN WESLEY (adapted)

*Prayer covers the whole of a man's life. There is no
thought, feeling, yearning, or desire, however low,
trifling, or vulgar we may deem it, which, if it
affects our real interest or happiness, we may not
lay before God and be sure of sympathy. His nature
is such that our often coming does not tire him. The
whole burden of the whole life of every man may be
rolled on to God and not weary him, though it has
wearied the man.*   HENRY WARD BEECHER

My heart is not proud, O LORD. . . . But I have stilled and quieted my soul; like a weaned child with its mother.   PSALM 131:1-2

I CONFESS, O God—
    that often I let my mind wander down
       unclean and forbidden ways:
  that often I deceive myself as to where my
       plain duty lies:
  that often, by concealing my real motives, I
       pretend to be better than I am:
  that often my honesty is only a matter
       of policy:
  that often my affection for my friends is only a
       refined form of caring for myself:
  that often my sparing of my enemy is due to
       nothing more than cowardice:
  that often I do good deeds only that they be
       seen of men, and shun evil
  ones only because I fear they may be found out.
  O holy One, let the fire of Thy love enter my heart, and burn up all this coil of meanness and hypocrisy, and make my heart as the heart of a little child.   JOHN BAILLIE

He who ceases to pray ceases to prosper.
                                        WILLIAM GURNEY BENHAM

Let us go to his dwelling place; let us worship at his footstool—arise, O LORD, and come to your resting place, you and the ark of your might.

PSALM 132:7-8

O THOU beloved: Love eternal, my whole good, happiness which has no bounds, I desire to appropriate you with the most vehement desire and the most worthy reverence. I desire to reserve nothing unto myself.

O everlasting light, surpassing all created luminaries, flash forth thy lightning from above, piercing all the most inward parts of my heart.

Make clean, make glad, make bright, and make alive my spirit, with all the powers thereof, that I may cleave to you in ecstasies of joy.

THOMAS À KEMPIS

I pray on the principle that wine knocks the cork out of a bottle. There is an inward fermentation, and there must be a vent.   HENRY WARD BEECHER

How good and pleasant it is when brothers live together in unity! It is like precious oil poured on the head, running down on the beard.

PSALM 133:1-2

BE PLEASED to visit your Church with the Holy Spirit. Renew the day of Pentecost in our midst, and in the midst of all gatherings of your people, may there come the downfall of the holy fire, the uprising of the heavenly wind. May matters that are now slow and dead become quick and full of life, and may the Lord Jesus Christ be exalted in the midst of his Church which is his fullness—"the fullness of him that filleth all in all." May multitudes be converted; may they come flocking to Christ with holy eagerness to find in him a refuge as the doves fly to their dovecotes.

CHARLES H. SPURGEON

In the morning, prayer is the key that opens to us the treasures of God's mercies and blessings; in the evening, it is the key that shuts us up under His protection and safeguard.   ANONYMOUS

Praise the LORD, all you servants of the LORD. . . .
Lift up your hands in the sanctuary and praise the
LORD.   PSALM 134:1-2

*L*ORD JESUS, today my son came to the breakfast table displaying the laces in his shoes. He had tied them by himself for the first time. He learned to do this so quickly, Lord; he's growing too fast for me.

For fun I sometimes ask him to stop growing because I love him just as he is. He protests that he can't stop growing.

So Lord, this is my prayer for him—that he would not stop growing; that throughout his life, long past the day of my death, he would continue to grow in grace; that the curtains of his tents would be stretched out, his cords lengthened, and his stakes strengthened.

Like you as a youth may he grow in favor with God and man; may he increase in wisdom and in years and become a man enlarged in his spirit and his heart.

Do this, O Lord, and give me the wisdom and the way to redeem the brief time he and I are together. Amen.   DANIEL PARTNER

Keep alert and always persevere in supplication for
all the saints.   EPHESIANS 6:18, *NRSV*

Praise the LORD, for the LORD is good; sing praise to his name, for that is pleasant.   PSALM 135:3

FATHER! It is your will that your child should enjoy your presence and blessing. It is your will that everything in the life of your child should be in accordance with your will, and that the Holy Spirit should work this in him. It is your will that your child should live in the daily experience of distinct answers to prayer, so as to enjoy living and direct fellowship with yourself. It is your will that your name should be glorified in and through your children, and that it will be in those who trust you. O my Father! Let this your will be my confidence is all I ask.   ANDREW MURRAY

If you are swept off your feet, it's time to get on your knees.   FRED BECK

Give thanks to the LORD, for he is good. His love endures forever. PSALM 136:1

GIVE US open eyes, our Father, to see the beauty all around us and to see it in Thy handiwork. Let all lovely things fill us with gladness and let them lift up our hearts in true worship.

Give us this day, O Lord, a strong and vivid sense that Thou art by our side. By Thy grace, let us go nowhere this day where Thou canst not come nor court any companionship that would rob us of Thine. Through Jesus Christ our Lord. Amen. PETER MARSHALL

Give us Lord, a bit o' sun,
A bit o' work and a bit o' fun;
Give us all in the struggle and sputter
Our daily bread and a bit o' butter.
ON AN OLD INN, LANCASTER, ENGLAND

By the rivers of Babylon we sat down and wept
when we remembered Zion . . . for there our captors
asked us for songs, our tormentors demanded songs
of joy.   PSALM 137:1, 3

*L*ORD, You told the impotent man
To take up his bed and walk.
Today, when mountainous problems
Seem to loom sky-high
        And the business of living
Demands so much rigid attention
Empower me, I pray
To take up my task and work.

                              RUTH HARMS CALKIN

Faith, and hope, and patience and all the strong,
beautiful, vital forces of piety are withered and
dead in a prayerless life. The life of the individual
believer, his personal salvation, and personal
Christian graces have their being, bloom, and
fruitage in prayer.   E. M. BOUNDS

May all the kings of the earth praise you, O Lord,
when they hear the words of your mouth. May they
sing of the ways of the Lord, for the glory of the
Lord is great.   PSALM 138:4-5

DEAR GOD and Father of my Lord Jesus Christ, you are blessed. You are the Father of mercies and God of all comfort who comforts me in all my troubles. You do this so that I may be able to comfort those who are in any trouble with the comfort with which I myself am comforted by you. Just as I share abundantly in the sufferings of Christ, thank you that my comfort is also abundant through Christ.   2 CORINTHIANS 1:3-5 (adapted)

All earth-born hopes with time must pass away;
Prayer grasps eternal things; pray, always pray.
                                        A. B. SIMPSON

O Lord, you have searched me and you know me.
You know when I sit and when I rise; you perceive
my thoughts from afar.   PSALM 139:1-2

ETERNAL and most glorious God, you
have stamped the soul of humanity with
your image, received it into your revenue, and made it part of your treasure; do not
allow us to undervalue ourselves, so to impoverish
you as to give away these souls for nothing, and
all the world is nothing if the soul must be given
for it. Do this, O God, for his sake who knows
our natural infirmities, for he had them, and
knows the weight of our sins, for he paid a dear
price for them; your Son, our Savior Jesus
Christ.   JOHN DONNE

Do you know what is wrong with the world today?
There's too much theologian and not enough
kneeologian.   DALLAS F. BILLINGTON

O Lord, I say to you, "You are my God." Hear,
O Lord, my cry for mercy.   PSALM 140:6

*B*LESSED are all your saints, O God and King, who have travelled over the tempestuous sea of this mortal life, and have made the harbor of peace and happiness. Watch over us who are still in our dangerous voyage; and remember such as lie exposed to the rough storms of trouble and temptations. Frail is our vessel, and the ocean is wide; but as in your mercy you have set our course, so steer the vessel of our life toward the everlasting shore of peace. Bring us at length to the quiet haven of our heart's desire, where you, O our God, are blessed, and live and reign for ever and ever.

AUGUSTINE

O, do not pray for easy lives. Pray to be stronger
men. Do not pray for tasks equal to your powers.
Pray for powers equal to your tasks.

PHILLIPS BROOKS

*O LORD, I call to you; come quickly to me. Hear my
voice when I call to you.*   PSALM 141:1

I NEED THEE, precious Jesus!
    I need a friend like thee;
    A friend to soothe and comfort,
  A friend to care for me:
I need the heart of Jesus,
    To feel each anxious care,
To bear my every burden,
    And all my sorrow share.

I need thee, precious Jesus!
    I need thee day by day,
To fill me with thy fullness,
    To lead me on my way;
I need thy Holy Spirit
    To teach me what I am;
To show me more of Jesus,
    To point me to the Lamb.   F. WHITFIELD

*It is impossible to conduct your life as a disciple
without definite times of secret prayer.*
                              OSWALD CHAMBERS

I cry aloud to the LORD; I lift up my voice to the LORD for mercy. I pour out my complaint before him; before him I tell my trouble.   PSALM 142:1-2

*O*GOD, renew our spirits by your Holy Spirit, and draw our hearts unto yourself, that our work may not be a burden, but a delight. Let us not serve as slaves with the spirit of bondage, but with freedom and gladness as your sons, rejoicing in your will; for Jesus Christ's sake.   BENJAMIN JENKS

Prayer is the soul's sincere desire,
*   Uttered, or unexpressed;*
The motion of a hidden fire
*   That trembles in the breast.*
                              JAMES MONTGOMERY

O Lord, hear my prayer, listen to my cry for mercy;
in your faithfulness and righteousness come to my
relief.   PSALM 143:1

ALMIGHTY FATHER, teach me to do everything with the utmost sincerity. Save me from posing even to myself. Make my life unaffected, simple, and sincere. Cleanse me from selfishness; let my gaze be outward rather than inward. Teach me to think more of others than of myself. Forbid that my own interests should be paramount. Pardon, I beseech you, all that is and has been wrong in my life and character. Had I always sought your will I should now have been strong in the Lord. But it is never too late. Help me to remedy the evil and henceforth to build with honesty and prayer.   WALTER JAMES

When you cannot pray as you would, pray as you
can.   EDWARD M. GOULBURN

O Lᴏʀᴅ, what is man that you care for him, the son of man that you think of him? Man is like a breath; his days are like a fleeting shadow.   PSALM 144:3-4

AS THE HAND is made for holding and the eye for seeing, you have fashioned me for joy. Share with me the vision that shall find it everywhere: in the wild violet's beauty; in the lark's melody; in the face of a steadfast man; in a child's smile; in a mother's love; in the purity of Jesus.   A GAELIC PRAYER

To get nations back on their feet, we must get down on our knees first.
    A LETTER TO THE EDITOR, the *Des Moines Register*

Great is the LORD and most worthy of praise; his greatness no one can fathom. PSALM 145:3

NOTHING has been capable, dear Lord, to hinder you from being all mine, neither heaven, nor your divinity, nor the gibbet of the cross: grant me the grace, that nothing may hinder me from being all yours, to whom I owe myself both for creation and redemption.

'Twas never heard that in your mortal life, you lodg'd with any, which you did not liberally reward with your gifts: I beg you will do the same to your present habitation, which is my heart: let the touch of yours, which consecrates all things, sanctify my heart that it may be grateful to you. LUCY HERBERT

Ah, dearest Jesus, holy Child,
Make thee a bed, soft, undefiled,
Within my heart, that it may be
A quiet chamber kept for thee. MARTIN LUTHER

Praise the LORD. *Praise the* LORD, *O my soul. I will praise the* LORD *all my life; I will sing praise to my God as long as I live.*   PSALM 146:1-2

O LORD JESUS CHRIST, you are the sun of the world, evermore arising, and never going down, which by your most wholesome appearing and sight, brings forth, preserves, nourishes, and refreshes all things, as well that are in heaven as also that are on earth; we beg you mercifully and faithfully to shine in our hearts, so that the night and darkness of sins, and the mists of errors on every side may be driven away; with you brightly shining in our hearts we may all our life space go without stumbling or offense, and may decently and seemly walk (as in the day time), being pure and clean from the works of darkness, and abounding in all good works which God has prepared us to walk in; you who with the Father and with the Holy Ghost live and reign for ever and ever.

                                    THOMAS CRANMER

Teach us to pray often; that we may pray oftener.
                                    JEREMY TAYLOR

*Praise the LORD. How good it is to sing praises to
our God, how pleasant and fitting to praise him!*
                                                    PSALM 147:1

O YOU, from whom to be turned is to fall,
         to whom to be turned is to rise,
         and in whom to stand is to abide for
    ever:
Grant us in all our duties your help
    in all our perplexities your guidance,
    in all our dangers your protection,
    and in all our sorrows your peace;
through Jesus Christ our Lord.   AUGUSTINE

To One alone my thoughts arise,
The Eternal Truth, the Good and Wise,
    To Him I cry,
Who shared on earth our common lot,
But the world comprehended not
    His deity.   HENRY WADSWORTH LONGFELLOW

Praise the LORD. Praise the LORD from the heavens, praise him in the heights above.   PSALM 148:1

O LORD, by all your dealings with us, whether of joy or pain, of light or darkness, let us be brought to you. Let us value no treatment of your grace simply because it gives us or denies us what we want; but may all that you send us bring us to you; that knowing your perfectness, we may be sure in every disappointment you are still loving us, in every darkness you are still enlightening us, and in every enforced idleness you are giving us life, as in his death you gave life to your Son, our Savior, Jesus Christ. Amen.   PHILLIPS BROOKS

Especially we pray you to make Christianity more Christian.   HARRY EMERSON FOSDICK

For the LORD takes delight in his people; he crowns the humble with salvation. Let the saints rejoice in this honor and sing for joy on their beds.

PSALM 149:4-5

*L*ORD, bless us, if it may be, in all our innocent endeavors. If it may not, give us the strength to encounter what is to come, that we be brave in peril, constant in tribulation, temperate in wrath and in all changes of fortune, and, down to the gates of death, loyal and loving one to another. As the clay to the potter, as the windmill to the wind, as children of their sire, we beg of you this help and mercy for Christ's sake.

ROBERT LOUIS STEVENSON

The answer of our prayers is secured by the fact that in rejecting them God would in a certain sense deny his own nature.   JOHN CALVIN

Praise the L*ORD*. *Praise God in his sanctuary; praise him in his mighty heavens.*   PSALM 150:1

O LORD GOD, praise your name for ever and ever! Yours is the mighty power and glory and victory and majesty. Everything in the heavens and earth is yours, O Lord, and this is your kingdom. I adore you as being in control of everything. Riches and honor come from you alone, and you are the Ruler of all mankind; your hand controls power and might and it is at your discretion that men are made great and given strength. O my God, I thank you and praise your glorious name, but who am I that I should be permitted to give anything to you? Everything I have has come from you, and I only give you what is yours already!   1 CHRONICLES 29:10-14 (adapted)

And take . . . the sword of the Spirit, which is the word of God; praying always with all prayer and supplication in the Spirit.

EPHESIANS 6:17-18, *NKJV*

*He [the righteous man] is like a tree planted by
streams of water, which yields its fruit in season
and whose leaf does not wither. Whatever he does
prospers.*   PSALM 1:3

YOU HAVE SAID that in virtue of your
going to the Father, whatever we ask,
you will do. . . . Blessed Lord! Forgive
me that I have so little believed you and your
promise, and so little proved your faithfulness in
fulfilling it. O forgive me that I have so little
honored your all-prevailing name in heaven or
upon earth.

Lord! Teach me to pray so that I may prove
that your name is indeed all-prevailing with God
and men and devils. Yea, teach me so to work
and so to pray that you can glorify yourself in me
as the Omnipotent One, and do your great
works through me too. Amen. ANDREW MURRAY

*We must hear Jesus speak if we expect him to hear
us speak.*   CHARLES H. SPURGEON

Therefore, you kings, be wise; be warned, you rulers of the earth. Serve the LORD with fear and rejoice with trembling.   PSALM 2:10-11

ALMIGHTY GOD, we make our earnest prayer that you will keep the United States in your holy protection; that you will incline the hearts of the citizens to cultivate a spirit of subordination and obedience to government, and entertain a brotherly affection and love for one another and for their fellow-citizens of the United States at large. And, finally, that you will most graciously be pleased to dispose us all to do justice, to love mercy, and to demean ourselves with that charity, humility, and pacific temper of mind which were the characteristics of the Divine Author of our blessed religion and without which we can never be a happy nation. Grant our supplications, we beseech you, through Jesus Christ our Lord. Amen.

GEORGE WASHINGTON

Indeed, I tremble for my country when I reflect that God is just.   THOMAS JEFFERSON

I lie down and sleep; I wake again, because the
LORD sustains me. I will not fear the tens of
thousands drawn up against me on every side.

PSALM 3:5-6

O MOST LOVING FATHER, you who will
us to give thanks for all things, to dread
nothing but the loss of yourself, and to
cast all our care on you, who care for us;
preserve us from faithless fears and worldly
anxieties, and grant that no clouds of this mortal
life may hide from us the light of that love which
is immortal, and which you have manifested
unto us in your Son, Jesus Christ our Lord.

WILLIAM BRIGHT

Prayer reaches out in love to a dying world and
says, "I care."   DICK EASTMAN

Answer me when I call to you, O my righteous God.
Give me relief from my distress; be merciful to me
and hear my prayer.   PSALM 4:1

D EAR FATHER, I've become your child,
        and your Son's Spirit
        is in my heart crying,
    "Abba! Father!"
I'm no longer enslaved to any law
    because I'm your child!
    And if I'm a child,
    I'm an heir through God.
Mine is not a spirit of slavery.
    I've received the Spirit of sonship.
    He cries within me, "Abba! Father!"
This Spirit speaks in mine, saying,
    "You're a child and heir;
        an heir of God,
        a joint heir with Christ!"
Abba, Father, if as an heir
I must suffer with your Son,
    these sufferings can't compare
        to the glory soon to be revealed in me.
                              DANIEL PARTNER

Prayer changes things.   ANONYMOUS

*But let all who take refuge in you be glad; let them
ever sing for joy. Spread your protection over them,
that those who love your name may rejoice in you.*
PSALM 5:11

WE BESEECH YOU, O God, the
God of truth,
That what we know not of things
we ought to know
You will teach us.
That what we know of truth
You will keep us therein.
That what we are mistaken in, as men must be,
You will correct.
That at whatever things we stumble
You will yet establish us.

And from all things that are false
And from all knowledge that would be hurtful,
You will evermore defend us,
Through Jesus Christ, our Lord.
BROOKE FOSS WESTCOTT

Praying is learned by praying.
L. A. T. VAN DOOREN

My soul is in anguish. How long, O LORD, how long? Turn, O LORD, and deliver me; save me because of your unfailing love.   PSALM 6:3-4

AND NOW, O God, give me a quiet mind, as I lie down to rest. Dwell in my thoughts until sleep overtake me. Let me rejoice in the knowledge that, whether awake or asleep, I am still with Thee. Let me not be fretted by any anxiety over the lesser interests of life. Let no troubled dreams disturb me, so that I may awake refreshed and ready for the tasks of another day. And to Thy Name be all the glory. Amen.   JOHN BAILLIE

The man who says his prayers in the evening is a captain posting his sentries. After that, he can sleep.   CHARLES BAUDELAIRE

O LORD my God, I take refuge in you; save and deliver me from all who pursue me, or they will tear me like a lion and rip me to pieces with no one to rescue me.   PSALM 7:1-2

O GOD in heaven, have mercy on us! Lord Jesus Christ, intercede for your people, deliver us at the opportune time, preserve in us the true genuine Christian faith, collect your scattered sheep with your voice, your divine Word as Holy Writ calls it. Help us to recognize your voice, help us not to be allured by the madness of the world, so that we may never fall away from you, O Lord Jesus Christ.   ALBRECHT DÜRER

Other duties become pressing and absorbing and crowd out prayer. "Choked to death" would be the coroner's verdict in many cases of dead praying if an inquest could be secured on this dire, spiritual calamity.   E. M. BOUNDS

When I consider your heavens, the work of your fingers, the moon and the stars, which you have set in place, what is man that you are mindful of him, the son of man that you care for him? PSALM 8:3-4

O GRACIOUS FATHER, keep me through your Holy Spirit; keep my heart soft and tender now in health and amidst the bustle of the world; keep the thought of yourself present to me as my Father in Jesus Christ; and keep alive in me a spirit of love and meekness to all, that I may be at once gentle and active and firm. O strengthen me to bear pain or sickness, or danger, or whatever you shall be pleased to lay upon me, as Christ's soldier and servant: and let my faith overcome the world daily. Perfect and bless the works of your Spirit in the hearts of all your people, and may your kingdom come and your will be done in earth as it is in heaven.   THOMAS ARNOLD

Do not work so hard for Christ that you have no strength to pray, for prayer requires strength.
                                   J. HUDSON TAYLOR

The LORD reigns forever; he has established his throne for judgment. He will judge the world in righteousness; he will govern the peoples with justice.   PSALM 9:7-8

LORD GOD, let us keep your Scriptures in mind and meditate on them day and night, persevering in prayer, always on the watch. We beg you, Lord, to give us real knowledge of what we read and to show us not only how to understand it, but how to put it into practice, so that we may deserve to obtain spiritual grace, enlightened by the law of the Holy Spirit, through Jesus Christ our Lord, whose power and glory will endure throughout all ages. Amen.   ORIGEN OF ALEXANDRIA

Of all things, guard against neglecting God in the secret place of prayer.   WILLIAM WILBERFORCE

O LORD, see how my enemies persecute me! Have mercy and lift me up from the gates of death, that I may declare your praises.   PSALM 9:13-14

O MY GOD, let me, with thanksgiving, remember, and confess unto you your mercies on me. Let my bones be bedewed with your love, and let them say unto you, who is like unto you, O Lord? You have broken my bonds in pieces. I will offer to you the sacrifice of thanksgiving. And how you have broken them, I will declare; and all who worship you, when they hear this, will say, "Blessed is the Lord, in Heaven and in earth, great and wonderful is his name."   AUGUSTINE

And since He bids me seek His face,
Believe His word and trust His grace,
I'll cast on Him my every care,
And wait for thee, sweet hour of prayer.

W. W. WALFORD

But you, O God, do see trouble and grief; you consider it to take it in hand. The victim commits himself to you; you are the helper of the fatherless.

PSALM 10:14

GRANT US GRACE, O Father, not to pass by suffering or joy without eyes to see; give us understanding and sympathy; and guard us from selfishness that we may enter into the joys and sufferings of others; use us to gladden and strengthen those who are weak and suffering; that by our lives we may help others who believe and serve you, and project your light which is the light of life.

H. R. L. SHEPPARD

God's promises are to be our pleas in prayer.

MATTHEW HENRY

You hear, O LORD, the desire of the afflicted; you encourage them, and you listen to their cry.

PSALM 10:17

O GOD, take all my sorrows and use them to show me the nature of your joy. Take all my sins and, forgiving them, use them to show me the ways of true pleasantness and the path of true peace. Take all my broken purposes and disappointed hopes and use them to make your perfect rainbow arch. Take all my clouds of sadness and calamity and from them make your sunset glories. Take my night and make it bright with stars. Take my ill-health and pain until they accomplish in your purpose as much as health could achieve. Take us as we are with impulses, strivings, longings so often frustrated and thwarted. And even with what is broken and imperfect, make your dreams come true, through him who made of human life a sacrament, of thorns a crown, of a cross a throne, even through Jesus Christ our Lord.

LESLIE D. WEATHERHEAD (adapted)

I have to hurry all day to get time to pray.

MARTIN LUTHER

For the LORD is righteous, he loves justice; upright men will see his face.   PSALM 11:7

O INFINITE GOD, the brightness of whose face is often shrouded from my mortal gaze, I thank Thee that Thou didst send Thy Son Jesus Christ to be a light in a dark world. O Christ, Thou Light of Light, I thank Thee that in Thy most holy life Thou didst pierce the eternal mystery as with a great shaft of heavenly light, so that in seeing Thee we see Him whom no man hath seen at any time.

And if still I cannot find Thee, O God, then let me search my heart and know whether it is not rather I who am blind than Thou who art obscure, and I who am fleeing from Thee rather than Thou from me: and let me confess these my sins before Thee and seek Thy pardon in Jesus Christ my Lord. Amen.   JOHN BAILLIE

God's chief gift to those who seek him is himself.
                                              E. B. PUSEY

"Because of the oppression of the weak and the groaning of the needy, I will now arise," says the LORD. *"I will protect them from those who malign them."*   PSALM 12:5

LORD JESUS, bless all who serve us, who have dedicated their lives to the ministry of others—all the teachers of our schools who labor so patiently with so little appreciation; all who wait upon the public, the clerks in the stores who have to accept criticism, complaints, bad manners, selfishness at the hands of a thoughtless public. Bless the mailmen, the drivers of streetcars and buses who must listen to people who lose their tempers.

Bless every humble soul who, in these days of stress and strain, preaches sermons without words. In the name of Him who called us to be the servants of all. Amen.   PETER MARSHALL

What is the life of a Christian but a life of prayer?
                                        DAVID BROWN

But I trust in your unfailing love; my heart rejoices in your salvation. I will sing to the LORD, *for he has been good to me.*   PSALM 13:5-6

A S THIS day closes, dear heavenly Father, I come to You to thank You for Your unfailing love, which even during the darkness of night continues to shine upon me and those I love. The wrongs and mistakes that have marred my life again today show me plainly how much I need You in my everyday life. Pardon me for Jesus' sake, and take away every impure thought and wish. Make my heart right, and make my actions reflect Your love. I want to become more like Jesus, Your dear Son, who went about doing good. Heal the sick, relieve the suffering, strengthen the weak, recall the erring, curb the wicked, help the troubled, comfort the sorrowing, and give peace to the dying. O Lord, who does not sleep, keep me safe until morning comes again. In Jesus' name, amen.

MY PRAYER BOOK

Prayer requires more of the heart than of the tongue.   ADAM CLARKE

The LORD looks down from heaven on the sons of men to see if there are any who understand, any who seek God. All have turned aside, they have together become corrupt; there is no one who does good, not even one.   PSALM 14:2-3

DELIVER US, good Lord, from the excessive demands of business and social life that limit family relationship; from the insensitivity and harshness of judgment that prevent understanding; from domineering ways and selfish imposition of our will; from softness and indulgence mistaken for love. Bless us with wise and understanding hearts that we may demand neither too much nor too little, and grant us such a measure of love that we may nurture our children to that fullness of manhood and womanhood, which you purposed for them, through Jesus Christ our Lord.

CHARLES S. MARTIN

I seldom made an errand to God for another but I got something for myself.   SAMUEL RUTHERFORD

LORD, who may dwell in your sanctuary? Who may live on your holy hill? He whose walk is blameless and who does what is righteous, who speaks the truth from his heart.   PSALM 15:1-2

GRANT ME, O most sweet and loving Jesus, to rest in you above every creature, above all health and beauty, above all glory and honor, above all power and dignity, above all knowledge and subtility, above all riches and arts, above all joy and exultation, above all fame and praise, above all sweetness and consolation, above all hope and promise, above all desert and desire, above all gifts and presents which you are able to bestow or infuse, above all joy and gladness which the mind is capable of receiving and feeling; finally, above angels and archangels, and above all the host of heaven, above all things visible and invisible, and above all that falls short of yourself, O you, my God!   THOMAS À KEMPIS

Prayer is the most difficult and costly activity of the Christian.   ALAN WALKER

I will praise the LORD, who counsels me; even at night my heart instructs me. I have set the LORD always before me. Because he is at my right hand, I will not be shaken.   PSALM 16:7-8

HEAVENLY FATHER, from whom all fatherhood in heaven and earth is named, bless, we beg you, all children, and give to their parents and to all in whose charge they may be, your Spirit of wisdom and love; so that the home in which they grow up may be to them an image of your kingdom, and the care of their parents a likeness of your love; through Jesus Christ our Lord.   LESLIE HUNTER

Prayer is a sincere, sensible, affectionate pouring out of the soul to God, through Christ, in the strength and assistance of the Spirit, for such things as God has promised.   JOHN BUNYAN

I call on you, O God, for you will answer me; give ear to me and hear my prayer. Show the wonder of your great love, you who save by your right hand those who take refuge in you from their foes.

PSALM 17:6-7

*L*ORD, educate us for a higher life, and let that life be begun here. May we be always in the school, always disciples, and when we are out in the world may we be trying to put into practice what we have learned at Jesus' feet. What he tells us in darkness may we proclaim in the light, and what he whispers in our ear in the closets may we sound forth upon the housetops.

CHARLES H. SPURGEON

Don't forget to pray for us too, that God will give us many chances to preach the Good News of Christ for which I am here in jail.   COLOSSIANS 4:3, *TLB*

I love you, O LORD, my strength. The LORD is my rock, my fortress and my deliverer; my God is my rock, in whom I take refuge. He is my shield and the horn of my salvation, my stronghold. PSALM 18:1-2

SOVEREIGN LORD, you are so good to me.
You are a stronghold in the day of trouble.
When trials come, where can I go but to you?
I have no other refuge.
O Christ, you are all I want.
Just and holy is your name.
Plenteous grace I find in you—grace that
            covers all my sin.
You are the fountain of life.
You satisfy all my longings.
I praise and exalt you from the depths of my heart.
                                    ROBERT C. SAVAGE

Real prayer seeks an audience and an answer.
                                    WILLIAM S. PLUMER

*As for God, his way is perfect; the word of the LORD
is flawless. He is a shield for all who take refuge in
him.*   PSALM 18:30

I HAVE much need of humbling myself
before You, the great and holy God,
because of the sins that I am daily guilty of
in thought, word, and deed against Your divine
majesty. Help me to overcome habitual levity in
my thoughts and to shun vain and impure
thoughts which, though they do not make their
abode in my mind for any long period of time,
yet in their passing through, often leave a
tincture of impurity.

Enable me to keep my heart with all diligence,
my thoughts and affections, for out of them are
the issues of life. How often have I offended in
this kind! Cleanse me from secret faults, for out
of the abundance of the heart the mouth speaks.
Help me to guard against vain and unnecessary
words, and to speak of You, my God, with that
reverence, that humility, that gravity that I
ought. Amen.   SUSANNA WESLEY

Cold prayers shall never have any warm answers.
                                           THOMAS BROOKS

You exalted me above my foes; from violent men you rescued me. Therefore I will praise you among the nations, O LORD; I will sing praises to your name.   PSALM 18:48-49

DEAR GOD and Father of my Lord Jesus Christ, you are blessed! By your great mercy I have been given a new birth into a living hope through the resurrection of Jesus Christ from the dead. There is now an inheritance which is imperishable, undefiled, and unfading, kept in heaven for me. By God's power I am protected through faith for a salvation that is ready to be revealed in the last time. Now I rejoice in thanksgiving for your mercy, this hope, and my inheritance and salvation.   1 PETER 1:3-6 (adapted)

God's ear lies close to the believer's lip.
                              ANONYMOUS

May the words of my mouth and the meditation of my heart be pleasing in your sight, O LORD, my Rock and my Redeemer.   PSALM 19:14

O DIVINE Master,
   Grant that I may not so much seek
      to be consoled as to console;
to be understood as to understand;
to be loved as to love.

For it is in giving that we receive;
   it is in pardoning that we are pardoned;
   and it is in dying that we are born to
            eternal life.   FRANCIS OF ASSISI

Prayer is the acid test of devotion.
                              SAMUEL CHADWICK

Some trust in chariots and some in horses, but we trust in the name of the LORD our God.

PSALM 20:7

L ORD
You want me to trust You so totally
That I am unmoved by any circumstance:
Then work in me that steadfast trust.
You want me to choose to do right:
Then turn me from wanting any plan but
          Yours.
You want me to revere and honor You:
Then refresh and revive me.
You want me to obey You uninterruptedly:
Then reassure me that Your promises are mine.
You want Your will to be my will:
Then help me to love Your every wish.

I expect Your help, dear Lord
For You've never broken a single promise
And You're not going to start with me.

RUTH HARMS CALKIN

God can pick sense out of a confused prayer.

RICHARD SIBBES

Be exalted, O LORD, in your strength; we will sing and praise your might.   PSALM 21:13

O GOD, Creator of all things, you are perpetually renewing the face of the world and have created us new in Jesus Christ; grant that in our worship of you and in communion with you, your created energy may more and more flood our lives, so that we may play our part in the fulfillment of your purpose, which transcends all that we can think or understand. Amen.   WILLEM VISSER 'T HOOFT

I would rather stand against the cannons of the wicked than against the prayers of the righteous.
                                        THOMAS LYE

In you our fathers put their trust; they trusted and you delivered them. They cried to you and were saved; in you they trusted and were not disappointed. PSALM 22:4-5

O LORD GOD, grant us always, whatever the world may say, to content ourselves with what you will say, and to care only for your approval, which will outweigh all words. CHARLES GORDON

I said, "Let me walk in the fields."
He said, "Nay, walk in the town."
I said, "There are no flowers there."
He said, "No flowers, but a crown."

I said, "But the sky is black,
There is nothing but noise and din."
But he wept as he sent me back—
"There is more," he said, "there is sin."

GEORGE MACDONALD

All the ends of the earth will remember and turn to the Lord, and all the families of the nations will bow down before him, for dominion belongs to the Lord and he rules over the nations.

PSALM 22:27-28

O LORD of changeless power and endless life, be favorable to your Church throughout the world. Gather, enlighten, sanctify and sustain it by your Holy Spirit. Give us more and more to trust the silent working of your perpetual grace, which brings forth in Christ the salvation of humanity. And let the whole world know that the things which were cast down are being raised up, and the things which had grown old are being made new, and all the things are returning to the perfection of him from whom they came. Amen.   PETER TAYLOR FORSYTH

No answer to prayer is an indication of our merit; every answer to prayer is an indication of God's mercy.   JOHN BLANCHARD

Even though I walk through the valley of the shadow of death, I will fear no evil, for you are with me; your rod and your staff, they comfort me.

PSALM 23:4

TAKE MY HAND, Lord, and lead me through this day, step by step. Remind me that I cannot do everything I wish, nor do any of it perfectly. Only you are perfect, and only with your help can I do my best. Help me to remember to ask for that help.

AVERY BROOKE

Never was a faithful prayer lost. Some prayers have a longer voyage than others, but then they return with their richer lading at last, so that the praying soul is a gainer by waiting for an answer.

WILLIAM GURNALL

*Lift up your heads, O you gates; lift them up, you
ancient doors, that the King of glory may come in.
Who is he, this King of glory? The LORD
Almighty—he is the King of glory.*   PSALM 24:9-10

CHRIST, whose glory fills the skies,
        Christ, the true and only light,
        Sun of Righteousness, arise,
    Triumph o'er the shades of night;
Dayspring from on high, be near;
Daystar, in my heart appear!

Visit, then, this soul of mine,
    Pierce the gloom of sin and grief;
Fill me, Radiancy Divine,
    Scatter all my unbelief;
More and more Thyself display,
Shining to the perfect day!   CHARLES WESLEY

*Jesus, remember me when you come into your
kingdom.*   LUKE 23:42, *NRSV*

Remember, O LORD, your great mercy and love, for
they are from of old. Remember not the sins of my
youth and my rebellious ways; according to your
love remember me, for you are good, O LORD.

PSALM 25:6-7

O LORD, reassure me with your quickening Spirit; without you I can do
nothing. Mortify in me all ambition,
vanity, vainglory, worldliness, pride, selfishness,
and resistance from God, and fill me with love,
peace, and all the fruits of the Spirit. O Lord, I
know not what I am, but to you I flee for refuge.
I would surrender myself to you, trusting your
precious promises and against hope believing in
hope. You are the same yesterday, today, and for
ever; and therefore, waiting on the Lord, I trust
I shall at length renew my strength.

WILLIAM WILBERFORCE

When we make self the end of prayer, it is not
worship but self-seeking.   THOMAS MANTON

*Guard my life and rescue me; let me not be put to
shame, for I take refuge in you. May integrity and
uprightness protect me, because my hope is in you.*
                                        PSALM 25:20-21

ALMIGHTY GOD, my heavenly Father,
who declares your glory and shows your
handiwork in the heavens and in the
earth; please deliver me from the service of
mammon, that I may do the work which you
give me to do, in truth, in beauty, and in
righteousness, with singleness of heart as your
servant, and to the benefit of my fellowmen; for
the sake of him who came as one that serves,
your Son Jesus Christ my Lord.

THE BOOK OF COMMON PRAYER (adapted)

*Hide me, O my Savior, hide,
Till the storm of life is past;
Safe into the haven guide,
O receive my soul at last!*   CHARLES WESLEY

Test me, O Lord, and try me, examine my heart and my mind; for your love is ever before me, and I walk continually in your truth.   PSALM 26:2-3

*L*ORD, teach me to ask in faith. I pray for wars to cease, but I am halfhearted because I don't believe man could stop being greedy so I think there will always be war. I pray that people may become more loving and tolerant to each other, but I don't really think that they will change. I pray for people to recover from their illnesses, or if they don't that they will grow more like you and will learn from their pain, but I ask halfheartedly, not believing.

Lord, increase my faith in you, in your goodness and love, and help me really to believe in your power to work in others and in myself. Save me from being cynical and give me faith as a grain of mustard seed which will grow and flourish. Jesus, I ask this in your name.

MICHAEL HOLLINGS and ETTA GULLICK

Unless I had the spirit of prayer, I could do nothing.
CHARLES G. FINNEY

One thing I ask of the LORD, this is what I seek: that I may dwell in the house of the LORD all the days of my life, to gaze upon the beauty of the LORD and to seek him in his temple.   PSALM 27:4

O GOD, who made of one blood all nations to dwell on the face of the whole earth and who sent your blessed Son to preach peace to those who are far off and to those that are near; grant that all everywhere may seek after you and find you. Bring the nations into your fold, pour out your Spirit upon all flesh, and hasten your kingdom; through the same, your Son, Jesus Christ our Lord.

GEORGE E. L. COTTON

The greatest need of foreign missions today is prayer.   R. A. TORREY

I am still confident of this: I will see the goodness of the LORD in the land of the living. Wait for the LORD; be strong and take heart and wait for the LORD.

PSALM 27:13-14

O BLESSED SPIRIT, have right of way in me this day. Help me to grow by the way of surrender. Let me lose my life that I may find it—in Thee. Give me power over the world, the flesh, and over all the devils of word or thought or deed. Teach me Thy strength; and when the night shall come, may I lie down in peace with Thee. Amen.

RALPH S. CUSHMAN

The one concern of the devil is to keep Christians from praying. He fears nothing from prayerless studies, prayerless work, and prayerless religion. He laughs at our toil, mocks at our wisdom, but trembles when we pray.   SAMUEL CHADWICK

*To you I call, O L*ORD *my Rock; do not turn a deaf ear to me. For if you remain silent, I will be like those who have gone down to the pit.*   PSALM 28:1

O H, what a terrible
Predicament I'm in!
Who will free me from my slavery
To this deadly lower nature?"

Lord, Paul's question
Is my question
But I'm sick of forever repeating the question.
Push me on
To the glorious answer:
"Thank God!
It has been done
By Jesus Christ our Lord.
He has set me free."

RUTH HARMS CALKIN, *Romans 7:25*

Prayer means that we have come boldly into the throne room and we are standing in His presence.
E. W. KENYON

The LORD sits enthroned over the flood; the LORD is enthroned as King forever. The LORD gives strength to his people; the LORD blesses his people with peace.   PSALM 29:10-11

O MY FATHER! I desire this day to walk before you with a good conscience, to do nothing that might grieve you or my blessed Lord Jesus. I ask you, may, in the power of the Holy Spirit, the cleansing in the blood be a living, continual, and most effectual deliverance from the power of sin, binding and strengthening me to your perfect service. And may my whole walk with you be in the joy of the united witness of conscience and your Spirit that I am well-pleasing to you. Amen.   ANDREW MURRAY

Whatever you do in revenge against your brother will appear all at once in your heart at the time of prayer.   THE DESERT FATHERS

You turned my wailing into dancing; you removed my sackcloth and clothed me with joy, that my heart may sing to you and not be silent.

PSALM 30:11

*L*ORD JESUS, remind me that you were born in the presence of farm animals, and that unlike the foxes and birds you had nowhere to lay your head. You prayed in the desert places, and when you sanctified the people with your blood you suffered outside the city gate. Lord, recall to my memory that Abraham lived in tents, as did Isaac and Jacob, while looking forward to the city which has foundations.

O Lord! I am too often seeking a continuing city today rather than looking for the city that is to come. Establish my heart among the heirs of the promise; those of whom the world was not worthy; those with a continual sacrifice of praise, the sweet fruit of lips that confess your name; the permanent residents of New Jerusalem, the city whose architect and builder is God.   DANIEL PARTNER

God shapes the world by prayer. Prayers are deathless. They outlive the lives of those who uttered them.   E. M. BOUNDS

Free me from the trap that is set for me, for you are my refuge. Into your hands I commit my spirit; redeem me, O LORD, the God of truth.

PSALM 31:4-5

M Y FAITH looks up to Thee,
Thou Lamb of Calvary,
Savior divine;
Now hear me while I pray;
Take all my guilt away;
O, let me from this day
Be wholly Thine!

May Thy rich grace impart
Strength to my fainting heart,
My zeal inspire;
As Thou hast died for me,
O may my love to Thee
Pure, warm, and changeless be,
A living fire!   RAY PALMER

Dealing in generalities is the death of prayer.

J. H. EVANS

Let your face shine on your servant; save me in your unfailing love. Let me not be put to shame, O LORD, for I have cried out to you.

PSALM 31:16-17

*L*ORD JESUS CHRIST, Sun of Righteousness, shine into my heart and life today. Help me to reflect Your light that someone who does not yet know You as Lord and Savior may be directed to You.

I thank You that You have carried the guilt of my sins. Let the sin and evil that may threaten today have no power over me. Grant me the grace to recognize Your will and the faith to do it. In all my dealings with others today, let me be guided by Your precept: "Whatever you wish that men would do to you, do so to them."

Keep me united with You as a branch of the true Vine, that I may draw from You the strength to abound in good works. May You be glorified today in all that I do; for Your name's sake, amen.

MY PRAYER BOOK

All who have walked with God have viewed prayer as the main business of their lives.

DELMA JACKSON

Love the LORD, all his saints! The LORD preserves the faithful, but the proud he pays back in full. Be strong and take heart, all you who hope in the LORD.   PSALM 31:23-24

GRANT US, our Father, your grace, that, seeing ourselves in the light of your holiness, we may be cleansed of the pride and vainglory which obscures your truth; and knowing that from you no secrets are hid, we may perceive and confront those deceits and disguises by which we deceive ourselves and our fellowmen. So may we worship you in spirit and in truth and in your light. Amen.

REINHOLD NIEBUHR

When the knees are not often bent, the feet soon slide.   ANONYMOUS

You are my hiding place; you will protect me from trouble and surround me with songs of deliverance. Rejoice in the LORD and be glad, you righteous; sing, all you who are upright in heart!

PSALM 32:7, 11

WE BRING before you, O Lord, the troubles and perils of people and nations, the sighing of prisoners and captives, the sorrows of the bereaved, the necessities of strangers, the helplessness of the weak, the despondency of the weary, the failing powers of the aged. O Lord, draw near to each; for the sake of Jesus Christ our Lord. Amen.   ANSELM OF CANTERBURY

We are never more like Christ than in prayers of intercession.   AUSTIN PHELPS

*Sing to him a new song; play skillfully, and shout
for joy. For the word of the LORD is right and true;
he is faithful in all he does.*   PSALM 33:3-4

WE MUST praise your goodness
that you have left nothing undone
to draw us to yourself. But one
thing we ask of you, our God, not to cease to
work in our improvement. Let us tend towards
you, no matter by what means, and be fruitful
in good works, for the sake of Jesus Christ our
Lord.   LUDWIG VAN BEETHOVEN

*From silly devotions
and from sour-faced saints,
good Lord, deliver us.*   TERESA OF AVILA

*May your unfailing love rest upon us, O LORD, even
as we put our hope in you.*   PSALM 33:22

FATHER I know now, if I never knew it
before, that only in Thee can my restless
human heart find any peace.

For I began life without knowledge, but full of
needs. And the turmoil of my mind, the
dissatisfaction of my life all stem from trying to
meet those needs with the wrong things and in
the wrong places.

Help me so to live that my conscience shall
not have to accuse, so that I may be saved the
necessity of trying to mend that which need
never be broken. I know that only then will the
civil war within me cease.

May I be willing to have Thee with me in play
as well as in work, knowing that with Thee I
shall have peace and joy and no regrets. Through
Jesus Christ, my Lord. Amen.

PETER MARSHALL

None can pray well but he that lives well.

THOMAS FULLER

Fear the LORD, you his saints, for those who fear him lack nothing. The lions may grow weak and hungry, but those who seek the LORD lack no good thing.   PSALM 34:9-10

O GOD, in whose one Gospel all are made one, let not your saving work fail in the broken order of Christendom because we have failed to understand your message. Prosper the labors of all churches bearing the name of Christ and striving to further righteousness and faith in him. Help us to place the truth above our conception of it, and joyfully to recognize the presence of the Holy Spirit wherever he may choose to dwell in human beings; through Jesus Christ our Lord.

CHARLES HENRY BRENT

So I tell you, whatever you ask for in prayer, believe that you have received it, and it will be yours.

MARK 11:24, NRSV

A righteous man may have many troubles, but the LORD delivers him from them all; he protects all his bones, not one of them will be broken.

PSALM 34:19-20

O GOD, my Father, who sent your Son to be my Savior; renew in me day by day the power of your Holy Spirit; that with knowledge and zeal, with courage and love, with gratitude and hope, I may strive powerfully in your service: may he keep my vision clear, my aspiration high, my purpose firm and my sympathy wide; that I may live as a faithful soldier and servant of my Lord Jesus Christ.

WILLIAM TEMPLE (adapted)

Prayer is the great engine to overthrow and rout my spiritual enemies, the great means to procure the graces of which I stand in hourly need.

JOHN NEWTON

My soul will rejoice in the LORD and delight in his salvation. My whole being will exclaim, "Who is like you, O LORD? You rescue the poor from those too strong for them, the poor and needy from those who rob them."   PSALM 35:9-10

*H*ELP us this day, we pray, to see the Christ
        Who died for the world,
Who came not to bring the righteous but
        sinners to repentance
Who came to love the lost, and save the
        sinful, and bring all men home to You.
And make us love with His Love until we too
        are burdened—
To preach the Gospel to the poor, to heal the
        brokenhearted,
To preach deliverance to the captives, and
        recovering of sight to the blind,
And to set all men at liberty until the
        kingdom comes.

                    ARTHUR A. ROUNER, JR.

The prayer that is faithless is fruitless.

                    THOMAS WATSON

*My tongue will speak of your righteousness and of
your praises all day long.*   PSALM 35:28

I AM INFLAMED, I am kindled by your gift;
and am carried upwards; I glow inwardly,
and go forwards. I ascend your ways that are
in my heart, and sing a song of degrees; I glow
inwardly with your fire, with your good fire, and
I go; because I go upwards to the peace of
Jerusalem: for I was gladdened in those who said
unto me, "We will go up to the house of the
Lord." Your good pleasure has placed us there,
that we may desire nothing else, but to abide
there forever.   AUGUSTINE (adapted)

*A sensible thanksgiving for mercies received is a
mighty prayer in the Spirit of God. It prevails with
Him unspeakably.*   JOHN BUNYAN

How priceless is your unfailing love! Both high and low among men find refuge in the shadow of your wings. They feast on the abundance of your house; you give them drink from your river of delights.

PSALM 36:7-8

GOD, when I am in need, or those I know and love are in need, it is easy to ask for your help. But it is more difficult to pray for strangers. Even when I know they are in great trouble, their needs seem very distant. Help me to imagine how they feel so that I may pray for them, not just with words but with my heart.

AVERY BROOKE

Selfishness is never so exquisitely selfish as when it is on its knees. . . . Self turns what would otherwise be a pure and powerful prayer into a weak and ineffective one.   A. W. TOZER

Commit your way to the Lord; trust in him and he will do this: He will make your righteousness shine like the dawn, the justice of your cause like the noonday sun.   PSALM 37:5-6

YOU ARE the God of peace who brought my Lord Jesus back from the dead. You are the great shepherd of the sheep. Because of the blood of the eternal covenant, equip me with everything good so that I may do your will. Work in me that which is pleasing in your sight, through Jesus Christ, to whom be the glory forever. Amen.

HEBREWS 13:20-21 (adapted)

When they had prayed, the place in which they were gathered together was shaken; and they were all filled with the Holy Spirit and spoke the word of God with boldness.   ACTS 4:31, NRSV

Turn from evil and do good; then you will dwell in the land forever. For the LORD *loves the just and will not forsake his faithful ones.*   PSALM 37:27-28

I THANK you for the peace and rest you give
          blessed Lord.
How amazing that even though you are
          totally omnipotent you are also meek
          and lowly in heart.
I exalt and worship you today because you
          make my yoke easy and my burden
          light.
Then you whisper, *Come unto me, all you who
          are weary and heavy-laden, and I will
          give you rest.*
You are so good to me.
Amen and amen!

                    ROBERT C. SAVAGE, *Matthew 11:28-30*

The Christian will find his parentheses for prayer even in the busiest hours of life.   RICHARD CECIL

The salvation of the righteous comes from the LORD;
he is their stronghold in time of trouble.

PSALM 37:39

MAKE ME a captive, Lord, and then I
shall be free;
Force me to render up my sword, and
I shall conq'ror be.
I sink in life's alarms when by myself I stand,
Imprison me within your arms, and strong
shall be my hand.
My heart is weak and poor until it master find:
It has no spring of action sure, it varies with the wind;
It cannot freely move till you have wrought
its chain;
Enslave it with your matchless love, and
deathless it shall reign.
My power is faint and low till I have learned
to serve:
It wants the needed fire to glow, it wants the
breeze to nerve;
It cannot drive the world until itself be driven;
Its flag can only be unfurled when you shall
breathe from heaven.

GEORGE MATHESON

Work as if everything depended upon work and
pray as if everything depended upon prayer.

WILLIAM BOOTH

O Lord, do not forsake me; be not far from me, O my God. Come quickly to help me, O Lord my Savior.   PSALM 38:21-22

I pray, O God, for all human hearts that today are lifted up to Thee in earnest desire, and for every group of men and women who are met together to praise and magnify Thy name. Whatever their mode of worship, be graciously pleased to accept their humble offices of prayer and praise, and lead them unto life eternal, through Jesus Christ our Lord. Amen.

JOHN BAILLIE

Elijah was as completely human as we are, and yet when he prayed earnestly that no rain would fall, none fell for the next three and a half years! Then he prayed again, this time that it would rain, and down it poured, and the grass turned green and the gardens began to grow again.   JAMES 5:17-18, *TLB*

But now, Lord, what do I look for? My hope is in you. Save me from all my transgressions; do not make me the scorn of fools.   PSALM 39:7-8

ALMIGHTY and Holy Spirit, the comforter, pure, living, true—illumine, govern, sanctify me, and confirm my heart and mind in the faith, and in all genuine consolation; preserve and rule over me so that, dwelling in the house of the Lord, all the days of my life, I may behold the Lord and praise him with a joyful spirit, and in union with all the heavenly church. Amen.   PHILIP MELANCHTHON

Prayer is the ascending vapor which supplies
The showers of blessing, and the stream that flows
Through earth's dry places, till on every side
"The wilderness shall blossom as the rose."
                                        A. B. SIMPSON

Many, O LORD my God, are the wonders you have done. The things you planned for us no one can recount to you; were I to speak and tell of them, they would be too many to declare.   PSALM 40:5

O Source of Life and Strength, many of Thy mercies do we plainly see, and we believe in a boundless store behind. No morning stars that sing together can have greater call than we for grateful joy. Thou hast given us a life of high vocation and Thine own breathing in our hearts interprets for us its sacred opportunities. Not a cloud of sorrow but Thou hast touched with glory; not a dusty atmosphere of care but that Thy light shines through. Let the time past suffice to have done our own will, and now make us consecrate to Thine. Amen.

JAMES MARTINEAU

It is in recognizing the actual presence of God that we find prayer no longer a chore, but a supreme delight.   GORDON LINDSAY

Yet I am poor and needy; may the Lord think of me.
You are my help and my deliverer; O my God, do
not delay.   PSALM 40:17

GOD, help me to remember that being alone is not the same as being lonely. Being alone, I'm in good company—I have many guests: You, first of all, then my good friends and the love they have for me, and then there's me. These times alone with just You and I together can be very wonderful, if I take advantage of them. I can get to know You and myself so much better. I can have rich conversations with You. I can learn from You how to live my life in a way that is pleasing to You. And I'd like to live that way, God. So, please sit down and visit awhile.   EMILY RICHTER

Because God is the living God, he can hear; because
he is a loving God, he will hear; because he is our
covenant God, he has bound himself to hear.
                                    CHARLES H. SPURGEON

Blessed is he who has regard for the weak; the LORD
delivers him in times of trouble.   PSALM 41:1

OH GOD—when I have food,
    Help me to remember the hungry;
    When I have work,
Help me to remember the jobless;
When I have a warm home,
Help me to remember the homeless;
When I am without pain,
Help me to remember those who suffer;
And remembering,
Help me to destroy my complacency,
And bestir my compassion.
Make me concerned enough to help,
By word and deed, those who cry out—
For what we take for granted.   ANONYMOUS

Prayers not felt by us are seldom heard by God.
                              PHILIP HENRY

*Why are you downcast, O my soul? Why so
disturbed within me? Put your hope in God, for I
will yet praise him, my Savior and my God.*

PSALM 42:11

I WILL SING to the LORD, for he
has triumphed gloriously;
horse and rider he has thrown into
the sea.
The LORD is my strength and my might,
and he has become my salvation;
this is my God, and I will praise him,
my father's God, and I will exalt him.
In your steadfast love you led the people
whom you redeemed;
you guided them by your strength to your
holy abode.
You brought them in and planted them on
the mountain of your own
possession,
the place, O LORD, that you made your abode,
the sanctuary, O LORD, that your hands
have established.
The LORD will reign forever and ever.

EXODUS 15:1-2, 13, 17-18, NRSV

*Let prayer be the key of the day and the bolt of the
night.*   JEAN PAUL RICHTER

Send forth your light and your truth, let them guide me; let them bring me to your holy mountain, to the place where you dwell. Then I will go to the altar of God, to God, my joy and my delight. I will praise you with the harp, O God, my God.

PSALM 43:3-4

*I*T'S HARD to be a man, today, God.
I don't know which way to go—tough guy or softie?
I can't act on instinct anymore,
    because it really isn't instinct after all, I'm told,
    but rather the way our fathers taught us to be.
But You must have had something in mind
                when You made a man, God.
Am I getting at all close to it?
    That's where I'd like to be.
    Maybe—even—something like Your Son—
    Who was quite a man.   MICHAEL BARROWS

Time spent in prayer is never wasted.

FRANCIS FENELON

I do not trust in my bow, my sword does not bring me victory; but you give us victory over our enemies, you put our adversaries to shame.

PSALM 44:6-7

ALMIGHTY and everliving God, who for the confirmation of the faith, allowed your holy apostle Thomas to be doubtful of your Son's resurrection: grant us so perfectly, and without all doubt, to believe in your Son, Jesus Christ, that our faith in your sight may never be reproved. Hear us, O Lord, through the same Jesus Christ, to whom with you and the Holy Spirit, be all honor and glory, now and forever more. Amen.   THOMAS CRANMER

No one is a firmer believer in the power of prayer than the devil; not that he practices it, but he suffers from it.   GUY H. KING

*We are brought down to the dust; our bodies cling
to the ground. Rise up and help us; redeem us
because of your unfailing love.*   PSALM 44:25-26

SHOW UNTO ME, O Lord, your mercy,
and delight my heart with it. Let me find
you, whom so longingly I seek.

See: here is the man whom the robbers seized,
and mishandled, and left half dead on the road
to Jericho. O you who can do what the kind-
hearted Samaritan cannot: come to my aid!

I am the sheep who wandered into the wilderness: seek after me, and bring me home again to
your fold. Do with me what you will, that all the
days of my life I may abide by you, and praise
you, with all those who are in heaven with you
for all of eternity. Amen.   JEROME

*He who has learned to pray has learned the
greatest secret of a holy and a happy life.*

WILLIAM LAW

Your throne, O God, will last for ever and ever; a scepter of justice will be the scepter of your kingdom.   PSALM 45:6

O LORD, come quickly and reign on your throne, for now often something rises up within me, and tries to take possession of your throne; pride, covetousness, uncleanness, and sloth want to be my kings; and then evil-speaking, anger, hatred, and the whole train of vices join with me in warring against myself, and try to reign over me. I resist them, I cry out against them and say, "I have no other king than Christ." O King of Peace, come and reign in me, for I will have no king but you! Amen.

BERNARD OF CLAIRVAUX

The devil enjoys hearing a prayer that is addressed to an audience.   ANONYMOUS

"Be still, and know that I am God; I will be exalted among the nations, I will be exalted in the earth." The LORD Almighty is with us; the God of Jacob is our fortress.   PSALM 46:10-11

GUIDE ME, O Lord, in all the changes and varieties of the world, that in all things that shall happen, I may have an evenness and tranquility of spirit, that my soul may be wholly resigned to your divine will and pleasure, never murmuring at your gentle chastisements and fatherly correction. Amen.

JEREMY TAYLOR

Many words do not a good prayer make; what counts is the heartfelt desire to commune with God, and the faith to back it up.   ANONYMOUS

For God is King of all the earth; sing to him a psalm of praise. God reigns over the nations; God is seated on his holy throne.   PSALM 47:7-8

*L*ORD, open my eyes so that I may see you; open my heart so I may experience your love. My eyes will be blinded by the vision of you, and my heart will be overwhelmed by the fire of your love. Let me not be afraid of dying to myself so that you may become my vision and the be-all and end-all of my life.

MICHAEL HOLLINGS and ETTA GULLICK

Time spent on the knees in prayer will do more to remedy heart strain and nerve worry than anything else.   GEORGE DAVID STEWART

Within your temple, O God, we meditate on your unfailing love. Like your name, O God, your praise reaches to the ends of the earth; your right hand is filled with righteousness.   PSALM 48:9-10

O THOU who changest not though all else changeth, abide with me. The years pass, the springtime changes into autumn, the shadows lengthen; help me to find the victory of each day and hour. And if, afar or near, I sometimes glimpse the valley of the shadow, deliver me, in Christ's dear Name, from all bondage of the fear of death. Help me to thrill forever with Eternal Spring.   RALPH S. CUSHMAN

But they that wait upon the LORD shall renew their strength; they shall mount up with wings as eagles; they shall run, and not be weary; and they shall walk, and not faint.   ISAIAH 40:31, KJV

Do not be overawed when a man grows rich, when the splendor of his house increases; for he will take nothing with him when he dies, his spendor will not descend with him.   PSALM 49:16-17

O LIGHT that never fades, as the light of day now streams through these windows and floods this room, so let me open to Thee the windows of my heart, that all my life may be filled by the radiance of Thy presence. Let no corner of my being be unillumined by the light of Thy countenance. Let there be nothing within me to darken the brightness of the day. Let the Spirit of Him whose life was the light of men rule within my heart till eventide. Amen.   JOHN BAILLIE

Is any among you afflicted? let him pray. Is any merry? let him sing psalms.   JAMES 5:13, KJV

He who sacrifices thank offerings honors me, and he prepares the way so that I may show him the salvation of God.   PSALM 50:23

GRACIOUS Lord, I thank You for Your Word of salvation, for it is a lamp unto my feet and a light unto my path. Grant that I may love it, understand it, believe it, and live according to it.

Make the Bible my comfort and guide. Open my heart and mind when I read Your Word that its sacred message may take root and grow. Help me to regard all faithful pastors and teachers as Your representatives, and strengthen my faith through their preaching and teaching.

Teach me to regard Sunday not only as a day of rest from my labors, but also as a day on which I may gladly hear and lean on Your holy Word.

Help me today, and at all times, to seek and find You as You have revealed Yourself in the Scriptures. Grant that I may daily worship and glorify You as my Creator, my Redeemer, and my Comforter; through Jesus Christ. Amen.

MY PRAYER BOOK

A wicked man in prayer may lift up his hands, but he cannot lift up his face.   THOMAS WATSON

Create in me a pure heart, O God, and renew a steadfast spirit within me. Do not cast me from your presence or take your Holy Spirit from me. Restore to me the joy of your salvation and grant me a willing spirit, to sustain me.   PSALM 51:10-12

CHANGE ME, God
Please change me.
Though I cringe
Kick
Resist and resent
Pay no attention to me whatever.
When I run to hide
Drag me out of my safe little shelter.
Change me totally
Whatever it takes
However long You must work at the job.
Change me—and save me
From spiritual self-destruction.

RUTH HARMS CALKIN

Prayer is not simply getting things from God, that is a most initial form of prayer; prayer is getting into perfect communion with God.

OSWALD CHAMBERS

I will praise you forever for what you have done; in your name I will hope, for your name is good. I will praise you in the presence of your saints.

PSALM 52:9

O LORD, I do groan and sigh when I think of the immense tasks and responsibilities you have laid on my shoulders because I know too well my failings and inadequacies. I groan and sigh, but I take hope in the promise that in my groans and confessions I am strengthened and forgiven and I am empowered and prayed for by your Spirit. I groan and I sigh, but I know full well that your yoke is easy and your burden is light compared to my trying to live and work without you. I praise you that I have experienced the difference between slavery in fear and service in friendship with you. May I never forget my need of your Spirit each moment of my life, and when I am groaning and sighing, may I be encouraged with the knowledge that you are there praying with me and for me through Jesus Christ my Savior. Amen.

LOUIS GIFFORD PARKHURST, JR.

The best prayers have often more groans than words.   JOHN BUNYAN

Oh, that salvation for Israel would come out of Zion! When God restores the fortunes of his people, let Jacob rejoice and Israel be glad!   PSALM 53:6

O GOD, who has made of one blood all nations of men to dwell on the face of the whole earth, and did send your blessed Son to preach peace to them that are far off and to them that are near; grant that all men everywhere may seek after you and find you. Bring the nations into your fold, pour out your Spirit upon all flesh, and hasten your kingdom; through your Son, Jesus Christ our Lord. Amen.
THE BOOK OF COMMON PRAYER

Prayer puts God's work in his hands—and keeps it there.   E. M. BOUNDS

I will sacrifice a freewill offering to you; I will praise your name, O LORD, for it is good.

PSALM 54:6

I GIVE you praise, O God, for a well-spent day. But I am yet unsatisfied, because I do not enjoy enough of you. I would have my soul more closely united to you by faith and love. I would love you above all things. You, who has made me, knows my desires, my expectations. My joys all center in you and it is you yourself that I desire; it is your favor, your acceptance, the communications of your grace that I earnestly wish for, more than anything in the world.

I rejoice in my relation to you, who are my Father, my Lord, and my God. I rejoice that you have power over me and that I desire to live in subjection to you. I thank you that you have brought me so far. I will beware of despairing of your mercy for the time which is to come, and will give you the glory of your free grace. Amen.

SUSANNA WESLEY

There must be fired affections before our prayers will go up.   WILLIAM JENKYN

Cast your cares on the LORD and he will sustain you; he will never let the righteous fall.

PSALM 55:22

THE LORD is my shepherd; I shall not want. He maketh me to lie down in green pastures: he leadeth me beside the still waters. He restoreth my soul: he leadeth me in the paths of righteousness for his name's sake. Yea, though I walk through the valley of the shadow of death, I will fear no evil: for thou art with me; thy rod and thy staff they comfort me.

Thou preparest a table before me in the presence of mine enemies: thou anointest my head with oil; my cup runneth over. Surely goodness and mercy shall follow me all the days of my life: and I will dwell in the house of the LORD for ever.   PSALM 23, *KJV*

It is impossible to lose your footing while on your knees.   ANONYMOUS

In God, whose word I praise, in the LORD, *whose word I praise—in God I trust; I will not be afraid. What can man do to me?*   PSALM 56:10-11

BLESSED FATHER! I thank you that the Holy Spirit is to me the bearer of the fullness of Jesus, and that in being filled with the Spirit I am made full with the fullness. I thank you that there have been people on earth since Pentecost, not a few, of whom you have said that they were full of the Holy Spirit. O my God! Make me full. Let the Holy Spirit take and keep possession of my deepest, inmost life. Let your Spirit fill my spirit. Let then the fountain flow through all the soul's affections and powers. Let it flow over and flow through my lips, speaking your praise and love. Let the very body, by the quickening and sanctifying energy of the Spirit, be your temple, full of the divine life. Lord my God! I believe you hear me. You have given it to me; I accept it as mine.

ANDREW MURRAY (adapted)

Answered prayers cover the field of providential history as flowers cover western prairies.

T. L. CUYLER

My heart is steadfast, O God, my heart is steadfast;
I will sing and make music. Awake, my soul!
Awake, harp and lyre! I will awaken the dawn.

PSALM 57:7-8

ETERNAL LIGHT, shine into my heart;
Eternal Goodness, deliver me from evil;
Eternal Power, be my support;
Eternal Wisdom, scatter the darkness of my
        ignorance;
Eternal Pity, have mercy upon me;
    that with all my heart and mind and soul and
            strength I may seek your face and be
            brought by your infinite mercy to your
            holy presence, through Jesus Christ
            our Lord.   ALCUIN OF YORK (adapted)

Be not hot in prayer and cold in praise.

ANONYMOUS

The righteous will be glad when they are avenged. . . . Then men will say, "Surely the righteous still are rewarded; surely there is a God who judges the earth."   PSALM 58:10-11

FILL THOU my life, O Lord my God,
In every part with praise
That my whole being may proclaim
Thy being and Thy ways.

Not for the lip of praise alone,
Nor even the praising heart,
I ask but for a life made up
Of praise in every part.

So shall no part of day or night
From sacredness be free;
But all my life, in every step,
Be fellowship with Thee.   HORATIUS BONAR

Do not want things to turn out as they seem best to you, but as God pleases. Then you will be free from confusion and thankful in prayer.

THE DESERT FATHERS

But I will sing of your strength, in the morning I will sing of your love; for you are my fortress, my refuge in times of trouble. O my Strength, I sing praise to you; you, O God, are my fortress, my loving God.   PSALM 59:16-17

O GOD! You are able to keep me from falling and to make me stand without a defect in the presence of your glory with rejoicing. You are the only God, my Savior. To you be glory, majesty, power, and authority, before all time and now and forever through Jesus Christ our Lord. Amen.

JUDE 1:24 (adapted)

I rise before the dawning of the morning and cry for help; I hope in your word.   PSALM 119:147, NKJV

Give us aid against the enemy, for the help of man is worthless. With God we will gain the victory, and he will trample down our enemies. PSALM 60:11-12

WHAT a choir this is, Lord, singing celestial harmonies in your praise.
Millions of angels blend their
voices in an exuberant tribute to you.
"Worthy is the Lamb that was slain!
Worthy is the Lamb that was slain!
Worthy to receive power and riches and wisdom and strength!
Worthy to receive honor and glory and blessing!"
My voice is lost in such a multitude, but
I worship you with heartfelt praise.
Thank you, thank you, blessed Jesus!

ROBERT C. SAVAGE, *Revelation 5:11-12*

Those who trade with heaven by prayer grow rich by quick returns.   WILLIAM S. PLUMER

For you have been my refuge, a strong tower against the foe. I long to dwell in your tent forever and take refuge in the shelter of your wings.

PSALM 61:3-4

ALMIGHTY GOD, you who have made all things for me, and me for your glory, sanctify my body and soul, my thoughts and my intentions, my words and actions, that whatsoever I shall think, or speak, or do, may by me be designed to the glorification of your name. And let no pride or self-seeking, no impure motive or unworthy purpose, no little ends or low imagination stain my spirit, or profane any of my words and actions. But let my body be a servant to my spirit, and both body and spirit servants of Jesus Christ.

THOMAS À KEMPIS (adapted)

Prayer, to the patriarchs and prophets, was more than the recital of well-known and well-worn phrases—it was the outpouring of the heart.

HERBERT LOCKYER

*Find rest, O my soul, in God alone; my hope comes
from him. He alone is my rock and my salvation; he
is my fortress, I will not be shaken.*   PSALM 62:5-6

FATHER, I will not ask for wealth or fame,
Though once they would have joyed my
carnal sense;
I shudder not to bear a hated name,
Wanting all wealth, myself my sole defense,
But give me, Lord, eyes to behold the truth,
A seeing sense that knows the eternal right;
A heart with pity filled and gentlest ruth;
A valiant faith that makes all darkness light;
Give me the power to labor for mankind;
Make me the mouth of such as cannot speak;
Eyes let me be to groping folk, and blind;
A conscience to the base; and to the weak
Let me be hands and feet; and to the foolish,
mind;
And lead still further on such as your kingdom
seek.   THEODORE PARKER

*God never denied that soul anything that went as
far as heaven to ask it.*   JOHN TRAPP

Because your love is better than life, my lips will glorify you. I will praise you as long as I live, and in your name I will lift up my hands. PSALM 63:3-4

USE ME, my Savior, for whatever purpose and in whatever way you may require. Here is my poor heart, an empty vessel: fill it with your grace. Here is my sinful and troubled soul; quicken it and refresh it with your love. Take my heart for your abode; my mouth to spread abroad the glory of your name; my love and all my powers for the advancement of your believing people; and never allow the steadfastness and confidence of my faith to abate.   DWIGHT L. MOODY

Let me burn out for God. After all, whatever God may appoint, prayer is the great thing. Oh, that I may be a man of prayer!   HENRY MARTYN

Let the righteous rejoice in the LORD and take refuge in him; let all the upright in heart praise him!

PSALM 64:10

OUR FATHER, I think of all the pain and heartache, the tears and sorrow, the greed and cruelty unloosed around the world. Help me to be an instrument of Thine to alleviate the pain, by this day:

returning good for evil,
returning soft answers for sharp criticisms,
being polite when I receive rudeness,
being understanding when I am confronted
by ignorance and stupidity.

So may I, in gentleness and love, check the hasty answer, choke back the unkind retort, and thus short-circuit some of the bitterness and unkindness that has overflowed Thy world. I ask this in the name of Jesus, who alone can give me the grace so to act. Amen.   PETER MARSHALL

Whether we like it or not, asking is the rule of the Kingdom.   CHARLES H. SPURGEON

You answer us with awesome deeds of righteousness, O God our Savior, the hope of all the ends of the earth and of the farthest seas, who formed the mountains by your power, having armed yourself with strength.   PSALM 65:5-6

I AM NOT worthy, Master and Lord, that you should come beneath the roof of my soul: yet since you in your love toward all wish to dwell in me, in boldness I come. You command, open the gates—which you alone have forged; and you will come in with love toward all as is your nature; you will come in and enlighten my darkened reason. I believe that you will do this: for you did not send away the harlot that came to you with tears; nor cast out the repentant publican; nor reject the thief who acknowledged your kingdom; nor forsake the repentant persecutor, a yet greater act; but all of those who came to you in repentance, were counted in the band of your friends, who alone abide blessed forever, now, and unto the endless ages.   JOHN CHRYSOSTOM

The great thing in prayer is to feel that we are putting our supplications into the bosom of omnipotent love.   ANDREW MURRAY

Say to God, "How awesome are your deeds! So
great is your power that your enemies cringe before
you. All the earth bows down to you; they sing
praise to you, they sing praise to your name."

PSALM 66:3-4

W E PRAY, O Lord, for deliverance
from all that weakens faith
in you:
from pompous solemnity;
from mistaking earnestness for trust in you;
from seeking easy answers to large questions;
from being overawed by the self-confident;
from dependence upon mood and feelings;
from despondency and the loss of self-respect;
from timidity and hesitation in making
decisions.
In Christ, we pray. Amen.   WILLARD SPERRY

Beyond our utmost wants
His love and power can bless;
To praying souls he always grants
More than they can express.   JOHN NEWTON

May the peoples praise you, O God; may all the peoples praise you. May the nations be glad and sing for joy, for you rule the peoples justly and guide the nations of the earth.   PSALM 67:3-4

ALMIGHTY GOD and heavenly Father, whose Son Jesus Christ was subject to Mary and Joseph at Nazareth, and shared there the life of an earthly home; send down your blessing, we beg you, upon all Christian families. Grant to parents the spirit of obedience and true reverence; and so bind each to each with the bond of mutual love, that to all its members of whatever age, every Christian family may be an image of the Holy Family of Nazareth.   EDWARD C. RATCLIFFE

The firmament of the Bible is ablaze with answers to prayer.   T. L. CUYLER

Sing to God, sing praise to his name, extol him who rides on the clouds—his name is the LORD—and rejoice before him.   PSALM 68:4

O GOD, who made us once a Christian people who strode to live by heaven's law, who loved Your Word in Scripture and in Psalm, who felt themselves privileged to worship every Sabbath day in the house of the Lord:

We have not loved You as our fathers loved. We have grown careless in our faith, and we have made worship in Your house a matter of convenience and not of conscience; a matter of comfort instead of sacrifice; a matter of fancy instead of faith.

Forgive us, Lord, that we think more of ourselves than we do of You. And forgive the Church in this land that before the world has seemed really to care so little. Give us a new heart, Lord, and a new spirit, we pray.

ARTHUR A. ROUNER, JR.

Prayer is a serious thing. We may be taken at our words.   DWIGHT L. MOODY

Sing to God, O kingdoms of the earth, sing praise to the Lord, to him who rides the ancient skies above, who thunders with mighty voice.

PSALM 68:32-33

O GOD of interstellar space, in whose sight a thousand years are as an evening gone; enlarge our horizons, we beg you, that we may behold your majesty in all your works and know your lordship in all your ways.

ROBERT N. RODENMAYER

Our prayers run along one road and God's answers by another, and by and by they meet.

ADONIRAM JUDSON

Answer me, O LORD, out of the goodness of your love; in your great mercy turn to me. Do not hide your face from your servant; answer me quickly, for I am in trouble.   PSALM 69:16-17

I DESIRE, O Lord, that you will, to all your other mercies, add that gift by which I shall trust in you—faith that works by love; faith that abides with me; faith that transforms material things, and gives them to me in spiritual meanings; faith that illumines the world by a light that never sets, that shines brighter than the day, and that clears the night quite out of my experience. I beg you to grant me this faith, that shall give me victory over the world and over myself; that shall make me valiant in all temptation and bring me off a conqueror and more that a conqueror through him that loved me. Amen.   HENRY WARD BEECHER

In our prayer time, there ought to be on our part a deep desire to have a conscience void of offense toward God and toward men.   PARIS REIDHEAD

I will praise God's name in song and glorify him with thanksgiving. This will please the LORD more than an ox, more than a bull with its horns and hoofs. PSALM 69:30-31

HOLY SPIRIT of God, who prefers before all temples the upright heart and pure, instruct us in all truth; what is dark, illumine; what is low, raise and support; what is shallow, deepen; that every chapter in our lives may witness to your power and justify the ways of God to men. In the name of Jesus, giver of all grace. Amen. JOHN MILTON

We must wrestle earnestly in prayer, like men contending with a deadly enemy for life.
J. C. RYLE

Yet I am poor and needy; come quickly to me,
O God. You are my help and my deliverer; O LORD,
do not delay.   PSALM 70:5

O UR FATHER, you made us. You made us so that we are restless until we rest in you. Accept, we beseech you, those pressure points in life where we know we need you. And help us. For you are our Father and we know who we are because you sent your Son, our brother, Jesus Christ. Amen.

JOHN B. COBURN

What a Friend we have in Jesus,
   All our sins and griefs to bear!
What a privilege to carry
   Everything to God in prayer!   JOSEPH SCRIVEN

Your righteousness reaches to the skies, O God, you who have done great things. Who, O God, is like you?   PSALM 71:19

HOW LOVELY is your dwelling place
      O LORD of hosts!
    My soul longs, indeed it faints
  for the courts of the LORD;
my heart and my flesh sing for joy
      to the living God. . . .

For a day in your courts is better
      than a thousand elsewhere.
I would rather be a doorkeeper in the house
      of my God
      than live in the tents of wickedness.
For the LORD God is a sun and shield;
      he bestows favor and honor.
No good thing does the LORD withhold
      from those who walk uprightly.
O LORD of hosts,
      happy is everyone who trusts in you.
          PSALM 84:1-2, 10-12, NRSV

I find in the Psalms much the same range of mood and expression as I perceive within my own life of prayer.   MALCOLM BOYD

*Praise be to the L*ORD *God, the God of Israel, who alone does marvelous deeds. Praise be to his glorious name forever; may the whole earth be filled with his glory. Amen and Amen.*

PSALM 72:18-19

O GOD, grant that looking upon the face of the Lord, as into a glass, I may be changed into his likeness, from glory to glory. Take out of me all pride and vanity, boasting and forwardness, and give me the true courage which shows itself by gentleness, the true wisdom which shows itself by simplicity, and the true power which shows itself by modesty.   CHARLES KINGSLEY (adapted)

A saint is to put forth his faith in prayer, and afterwards follow his prayer with faith.

VAVASOR POWELL

Whom have I in heaven but you? And earth has nothing I desire besides you. My flesh and my heart may fail, but God is the strength of my heart and my portion forever.   PSALM 73:25-26

ALMIGHTY GOD, it seems that the great people of earth are people who pray— not those who talk about prayer, nor those who say they believe in prayer, but those who take time to pray. Help me to be such a one, dear God, for my soul's sake and Thy Kingdom's sake. Amen.   RALPH S. CUSHMAN

The more praying there is in the world, the better the world will be; the mightier the forces against evil everywhere.   E. M. BOUNDS

Rise up, O God, and defend your cause; remember how fools mock you all day long. Do not ignore the clamor of your adversaries, the uproar of your enemies, which rises continually.   PSALM 74:22-23

*L*ORD JESUS, we are constantly shown on TV, in the newspapers, and in the movies the horrors of the world, the evil and perverted behavior of mankind, so that we come close to despair. You, Lord, in your life knew failure, saw men betray and torture each other. You knew hell on earth as we do, but you did not despair, for you loved men and trusted your Father.

Keep alight in our hearts the flame of hope, make us to see the beautiful and good things in the world, not just the drab, the squalid and sordid. Help us to see the goodness of men, and by our love increase this and make it grow and spread among the people, for we are your instruments in the world. Make your hope and love shine through us so that the hells of others may be lightened and they may glimpse something of your glory.

MICHAEL HOLLINGS and ETTA GULLICK

Revival fires flame where hearts are praying.

DICK EASTMAN

We give thanks to you, O God, we give thanks, for your Name is near; men tell of your wonderful deeds.   PSALM 75:1

I MOST humbly beg you to give me grace not only to be a hearer of the Word, but a doer also of the same; not only to love, but also to live your gospel; not only to favor, but also to follow your godly doctrine; not only to profess, but also to practice your blessed commandments, to the honor of your Holy Name, and the health of my soul.   THOMAS BECON (adapted)

If we do not love one another, we certainly shall not have much power with God in prayer.
                                    DWIGHT L. MOODY

*Make vows to the LORD your God and fulfill them;
let all the neighboring lands bring gifts to the One
to be feared. He breaks the spirit of rulers; he is
feared by the kings of the earth.*   PSALM 76:11-12

GRANT, Almighty God, since I have
already entered in hope upon the threshold of my eternal inheritance, and know
that there is a mansion for me in heaven since
Christ, my head and the firstfruits of my salvation, has been received there; grant that I may
proceed more and more in the way of your holy
calling until at length I reach the goal and so
enjoy the eternal glory of which you have given
me a taste in this world, by the same Christ my
Lord.   JOHN CALVIN

*Saints of the early church reaped great harvests in
the field of prayer and found the mercy seat to be a
mine of untold treasures.*   CHARLES H. SPURGEON

Your ways, O God, are holy. What god is so great as our God? You are the God who performs miracles; you display your power among the peoples.

PSALM 77:13-14

*O*LORD GOD, in whom we live and move and have our being, open our eyes that we may behold your fatherly presence ever about us. Teach us to be anxious for nothing, and when we have done what you have given us to do, help us, O God our Savior, to leave the issue to your wisdom, knowing that all things are possible to us through your Son our Savior, Jesus Christ. RICHARD MEUX BENSON

Prayer is a shield to the soul, a sacrifice to God, and a scourge for Satan.   JOHN BUNYAN

We will tell the next generation the praiseworthy deeds of the LORD, his power, and the wonders he has done.   PSALM 78:4

*B*LESS MY children with healthful bodies, with good understandings, with the graces and gifts of your Spirit, with sweet dispositions and holy habits, and sanctify them throughout in their bodies and souls and spirits, and keep them unblamable to the coming of the Lord Jesus.   JEREMY TAYLOR

Beware of the barrenness of a busy life.
                                     CORRIE TEN BOOM

Their hearts were not loyal to him, they were not faithful to his covenant. Yet he was merciful; he forgave their iniquities and did not destroy them.

PSALM 78:37-38

GIVE ME, O God,
A steadfast heart, which no unworthy
affection may drag downwards;
An unconquered heart, which no tribulation
can wear out;
An upright heart, which no unworthy
purpose may tempt aside.

THOMAS AQUINAS

The great thing in prayer is to feel that we are putting our supplications into the bosom of omnipotent love.   ANDREW MURRAY

*He chose David his servant and took him from the
sheep pens. . . . And David shepherded them with
integrity of heart; with skillful hands he led them.*

PSALM 78:70, 72

MAY THE strength of God pilot me. May
the power of God preserve me. May the
wisdom of God instruct me. May the
hand of God protect me. May the way of God
direct me. May the shield of God defend me.

PATRICK OF IRELAND (adapted)

*Bear up the hands that hang down, by faith and
prayer; support the tottering knees. Storm the
throne of grace and persevere therein, and mercy
will come down.*   JOHN WESLEY

Help us, O God our Savior, for the glory of your name; deliver us and forgive our sins for your name's sake.   PSALM 79:9

O GOD, as the day returns and brings us the petty round of irritating duties, help us to perform them with laughter and kind faces; let cheerfulness abound with industry; give us to go blithely on our business all this day; bring us to our resting beds weary and content and undishonored; and grant us in the end the gift of sleep.   ROBERT LOUIS STEVENSON

Prayer is the soul's breathing itself into the bosom of its heavenly Father.   THOMAS WATSON

Restore us, O God Almighty; make your face shine upon us, that we may be saved.   PSALM 80:7

O God, you made us in your own image and redeemed us through Jesus your Son: Look with compassion on the whole human family; take away the arrogance and hatred which infect our hearts; break down the walls that separate us; unite us in bonds of love; and work through our struggle and confusion to accomplish your purposes on earth; that, in your good time, all nations and races may serve you in harmony around your heavenly throne; through Jesus Christ our Lord. Amen.   THE BOOK OF COMMON PRAYER

Likewise you husbands, dwell with them with understanding, giving honor to the wife . . . that your prayers may not be hindered.
1 PETER 3:7, *NKJV*

"If my people would but listen to me, if Israel would follow my ways, how quickly would I subdue their enemies and turn my hand against their foes!"

PSALM 81:13-14

*I*N THE SWIRLS and swishes of life, dear God, we are carried by the currents, ducked by waves, tossed by the torrents, and sometimes float placidly with the tide's ebb and flow.

Amid all these swirls and swishes, give me a temperate spirit, a waiting spirit, a spirit not concerned to get my own way, not vindictive nor boiling with rage.

Keep my deepest instincts anchored in you so where the waves go and I go, I go in you. And we all are carried by the undercurrent of your love into eternity.   JOHN B. COBURN

God answers all true prayer, either in kind or in kindness.   ADONIRAM JUDSON

Defend the cause of the weak and fatherless. . . . Rescue the weak and needy; deliver them from the hand of the wicked.   PSALM 82:3-4

FORGIVE US, Lord, for not expecting You everywhere.
    O Jesus, especially forgive us for not expecting You in poor places—
    in unpainted houses, with weeds and high
        grass in front,
    in alleys and taverns, and all those places that
        aren't very nice.
We forget about the barn, Lord, and about
        the baby born among the beasts.
    It never occurred to us that a Young Prince
        of Peace would ever find His power
        by growing up in Nothingsville,
        in Dullsville!
And that He would be crowned with thorns
        and throned on a cross and win His
        battles with a sword of the Spirit!
O Lord we have so much to learn.
    Help us to see the light of the star today, and
        to hear the sound of a song, and learn
        the knowledge of a truth! Amen.

ARTHUR A. ROUNER, JR.

Prayer is the key that opens the door to all that is good in life.   ANONYMOUS

Let them [your enemies] know that you, whose name is the LORD—that you alone are the Most High over all the earth.   PSALM 83:18

MY GOD, I love you; not because
I hope for heaven thereby,
Nor yet because who love you not
Are lost eternally.

Not with the hope of gaining anything,
Not seeking a reward;
But as you have loved me,
O ever-loving Lord!

Even so I love you, and will love,
And in your praise will sing,
Solely because you are my God,
and my eternal King.

ANONYMOUS, Seventeenth Century

Many pray with their lips for that for which their hearts have no desire.   JONATHAN EDWARDS

*Better is one day in your courts than a thousand
elsewhere; I would rather be a doorkeeper in the
house of my God than dwell in the tents of the
wicked.*   PSALM 84:10

JESUS, you know what it is to be human and
that it is not easy to love our neighbor as
ourselves.

When we do not understand our neighbors,
nor they us, help us to think more about how we
could understand them and less about how they
could understand us. May we never let fear keep
us from speaking or acting in love, nor thought-
lessness spoil the impulse of the heart.

May we do all that we do in gratitude to you,
rather than in desire for praise, and when our
time, energy or talent are at an end, may we
quietly ask your help and remember that you
love and care for them much more than we do.

AVERY BROOKE

*The beginning of anxiety is the end of faith, and the
beginning of true faith is the end of anxiety.*

GEORGE MUELLER

Will you not revive us again, that your people may rejoice in you? Show us your unfailing love, O LORD, and grant us your salvation. PSALM 85:6-7

GIVE US, O Lord God, a deep sense of your holiness; how you are of purer eyes than to behold iniquity, and cannot overlook or pass by that which is evil.

Give us no less, O Lord, a deep sense of your wonderful love towards us; how you would not let us alone in our ruin, but did come after us, in the person of your Son, Jesus Christ, to bring us back to our true home with you.

Quicken in us, O Lord, the Spirit of gratitude, of loyalty and of sacrifice, that we may seek in all things to please him who humbled himself for us, even to the death of the cross, by dying unto sin and living unto righteousness; through the same Jesus Christ our Lord.   DEAN VAUGHAN

God tells us to burden him with whatever burdens us.   ANONYMOUS

Teach me your way, O LORD, and I will walk in your truth; give me an undivided heart, that I may fear your name.   PSALM 86:11

O GOD, You have glorified our victorious Savior with a visible, triumphant resurrection from the dead, and ascension into heaven, where he sits at your right hand; grant, we beg you, that his triumphs and glories may ever shine in our eyes, to make us endure our own; being assured by his example, that if we endeavor to live and die like him, for the advancement of your love in ourselves and others, you will raise our dead bodies again, and conforming them to his glorious body, call us above the clouds, and give us possession of your everlasting kingdom.   JOHN WESLEY

Prayer time must be kept up as duly as meat-time.
                                    MATHEW HENRY

Indeed, of Zion it will be said, "This one and that one were born in her, and the Most High himself will establish her." The LORD will write in the register of the peoples: "This one was born in Zion."

PSALM 87:5-6

O HEAVENLY Father,
I praise and thank you
For the peace of the night.
I praise and thank you for this new day.
I praise and thank you for all your goodness
and faithfulness throughout my life.
You have granted me many blessings;
Now let me also accept what is hard from your
        hand.
You will lay on me no more than I can bear.
You make all things work together for good for
        your children.

DIETRICH BONHOEFFER

I will pray morning, noon, and night.

PSALM 55:17, *TLB*

*But I cry to you for help, O LORD; in the morning
my prayer comes before you.*   PSALM 88:13

GRANT, O heavenly Father, that the
spiritual refreshment I have this day
enjoyed may not be left behind and forgotten as tomorrow I return to the cycle of common tasks. Here is a fountain of inward strength.
Here is a purifying wind that must blow through
all my business and all my pleasures. Here is
light to enlighten all my road. Therefore, O God,
do Thou enable me so to discipline my will that
in hours of stress I may honestly seek after those
things for which I have prayed in hours of peace.

JOHN BAILLIE

*O Lord, you know what is best for me. Let this or
that be done, as you please. Give what you will,
how much you will, and when you will.*

THOMAS À KEMPIS

The heavens praise your wonders, O LORD, your faithfulness too, in the assembly of the holy ones. For who in the skies above can compare with the LORD? Who is like the LORD among the heavenly beings?   PSALM 89:5-6

SHOW ME, O God, that the one great hindrance is my own wisdom, my imagination that I can understand the Word and Truth of God. Oh teach me to become a fool that I may be wise. May my whole life become one continued act of faith, that the Holy Spirit will surely do his work of teaching, guiding, and leading into the truth. Father, you gave him that he might reveal Jesus in his glory within me; I wait for this. Amen.   ANDREW MURRAY

We are going home to many who cannot read. So, Lord, make us to be Bibles so that those who cannot read the Book can read it in us.

AN UNKNOWN CHINESE WOMAN

Righteousness and justice are the foundation of your throne; love and faithfulness go before you. Blessed are those who have learned to acclaim you, who walk in the light of your presence, O LORD.

PSALM 89:14-15

ETERNAL FATHER, you alone can control the days that are gone and the deeds that are done; remove from my burdened memory the weight of past years, that being set free both from the glamour of complacency and from the palsy of remorse, I may reach forth unto those things which are before, and press towards the mark for the prize of the high calling of God in Christ Jesus.   CHARLES HENRY BRENT

Prayer is a strong wall and fortress of the church; it is a goodly Christian's weapon.

MARTIN LUTHER

How long, O LORD? Will you hide yourself forever?
How long will your wrath burn like fire? Remem-
ber how fleeting is my life. For what futility you
have created all men!   PSALM 89:46-47

WE BRING before you, O Lord, the
troubles and perils of people and
nations, the sighing of prisoners
and captives, the sorrows of the bereaved, the
necessities of strangers, the helplessness of the
weak, the despondency of the weary, the failing
powers of the aged. O Lord, draw near to each;
for the sake of Jesus Christ our Lord. Amen.

ANSELM OF CANTERBURY

A man's state before God may always be measured
by his prayers.   J. C. RYLE

If you make the Most High your dwelling—even the LORD, who is my refuge—then no harm will befall you, no disaster will come near your tent.

PSALM 91:9-10

GIVE, I pray you, to all children grace reverently to love their parents, and lovingly to obey them. Teach us all that filial duty never ends or lessens; and bless all parents in their children, and all children in their parents.   CHRISTINA ROSSETTI

All the prayers in the Scripture you will find to be reasoning with God, not a multitude of words heaped together.   STEPHEN CHARNOCK

The LORD reigns, he is robed in majesty; the LORD is robed in majesty and is armed with strength. The world is firmly established; it cannot be moved.

PSALM 93:1

THOUGH the fig tree does not blossom,
    and no fruit is on the vines;
    though the produce of the olive fails
and the fields yield no food;
though the flock is cut off from the fold
        and there is no herd in the stalls,
yet I will rejoice in the Lord; I will exult
        in the God of my salvation.
Lord, you are my strength; you make my
        feet like the feet of a deer,
and make me tread upon the heights.

HABAKKUK 3:17-19 (adapted)

*The LORD is far from the wicked,
    but he hears the prayer of the righteous.*

PROVERBS 15:29, *NRSV*

Blessed is the man you discipline, O LORD, the man you teach from your law; you grant him relief from days of trouble, till a pit is dug for the wicked.

PSALM 94:12-13

O GOD, we do not desire new contentions and discord. We pray only that the Son of God, our Lord Jesus Christ, who for us died and rose form the grave, will guide us, that all of us who are in many churches and many communions may be one Church, one Communion, and one in him. As he himself earnestly prayed for us in his hour of death, saying, "I pray also for those who through your Word will believe in me, that they may be one as you, Father, are in union with me and I with you, and that they may be one in us," so also we pray. Amen.   PHILIP MELANCHTHON

In Gethsemane the holiest of all petitioners prayed three times that a certain cup might pass from Him. It did not. After that the idea that prayer is recommended to us as a sort of infallible gimmick may be dismissed.   C. S. LEWIS

Declare his glory among the nations, his marvelous deeds among all peoples. For great is the LORD and most worthy of praise; he is to be feared above all gods.   PSALM 96:3-4

*O*UR FATHER which art in heaven, Hallowed be thy name. Thy Kingdom come. Thy will be done in earth, as it is in heaven. Give us this day our daily bread. And forgive us our debts, as we forgive our debtors. And lead us not into temptation, but deliver us from evil: For thine is the kingdom, and the power, and the glory, for ever. Amen.

MATTHEW 6:9-13, *KJV*

The Lord's Prayer may be committed to memory quickly, but it is slowly learnt by heart.

FREDERICK DENISON MAURICE

Light is shed upon the righteous and joy on the upright in heart. Rejoice in the LORD, you who are righteous, and praise his holy name.

PSALM 97:11-12

GRANT, O my God, that I may know you, love you and rejoice in you; and if in this life I cannot do these things fully, grant that I may at the least progress in them from day to day, for Christ's sake. Amen.

ANSELM OF CANTERBURY (adapted)

In the calm of sweet communion
  Let thy daily work be done;
In the peace of soul-outpouring
  Care be banished, patience won;
And if earth with its enchantments
  Seek thy spirit to enthrall,
Ere thou listen, ere thou answer,
  Turn to Jesus, tell Him all.   G. M. TAYLOR

The LORD reigns, let the nations tremble; he sits enthroned between the cherubim, let the earth shake. Great is the LORD in Zion; he is exalted over all the nations.   PSALM 99:1-2

*E*TERNAL Father, source of life and light, whose love extends to all people, all creatures, all things: Grant us that reverence for life which becomes those who believe in you; lest we despise it, degrade it, or come callously to destroy it. Rather let us save it, secure it, and sanctify it, after the example of your Son, Jesus Christ our Lord.

ROBERT RUNCIE

God is not a cosmic bellboy for whom we can press a button to get things.   HARRY EMERSON FOSDICK

*Know that the LORD is God. It is he who made us,
and we are his; we are his people, the sheep of his
pasture.*   PSALM 100:3

O LORD, keep us sensitive to the grace
that is around us. May the familiar not
become neglected. May we see your
goodness in our daily bread, and may the comforts of our home take our thoughts to the merci-
fulness of God. Through Jesus Christ. Amen.

J. H. JOWETT

*Even if no command to pray had existed, our very
weakness would have suggested it.*

FRANCIS FENELON

I will sing of your love and justice; to you, O LORD, I will sing praise. I will be careful to lead a blameless life—when will you come to me?

PSALM 101:1-2

O PRINCE of Life, teach me to stand more boldly on your side, to face the world and all my adversaries more courageously, and not to let myself be dismayed by any storm of temptation; may my eyes be steadfastly fixed on you in fearless faith; may I trust you with perfect confidence that you will keep me, save me, and bring me through by the power of your grace and the riches of your mercy.

GERHARD TERSTEEGEN (adapted)

The prayers of the Christian are secret, but their effect cannot be hidden.

HOWARD CHANDLER ROBBINS

In the beginning you laid the foundations of the earth, and the heavens are the work of your hands. They will perish, but you remain . . . the same, and your years will never end. PSALM 102:25-27

ALMIGHTY and most merciful God, you have given the Bible to be the revelation of your great love to us, and of your power and will to save us: grant that our study of it may not be made in vain by the callousness or carelessness of our heart, but that by it we may be confirmed in penitence, lifted to hope, made strong for service, and, above all, filled with the true knowledge of yourself and of your Son, Jesus Christ. GEORGE ADAM SMITH

If you can't pray as you want to, pray as you can. God knows what you mean. VANCE HAVNER

The LORD is compassionate and gracious, slow to anger, abounding in love. He will not always accuse, nor will he harbor his anger forever; he does not treat us as our sins deserve or repay us according to our iniquities.   PSALM 103:8-10

HELP ME, O God, to look back on the long way you have brought me, on the long days in which I have been served, not according to my deserts, but my desires; on the pit and the miry clay, the blackness of despair, the horror of misconduct, from which my feet have been plucked out. For my sins forgiven or prevented, for my shame unpublished, I bless and thank you, O God.

Help me yet again and ever. So order events, so strengthen my frailty, as that day by day I shall come before you with this song of gratitude, and in the end be dismissed with honor. In my weakness and in my fear, this vessel of your handiwork so prays to you, so praise to you. Amen.   ROBERT LOUIS STEVENSON (adapted)

Men of God are always men of prayer.
                                    HENRY T. MAHAN

Praise the LORD, O my soul. O LORD my God, you are very great; you are clothed with splendor and majesty.   PSALM 104:1

WE THANK YOU, Lord God, heavenly Father, for Your faithful providence which we have enjoyed and for Your gracious provision of fellowship with one another and with You. Teach us to receive Your gifts with thanksgiving, that with grateful hearts we may enjoy the gifts that have come from You, who together with the Son and the Holy Ghost are one God and one Lord. Amen.

MY PRAYER BOOK

We may as well not pray at all as offer our prayers in a lifeless manner.   WILLIAM S. PLUMER

I will sing to the LORD all my life; I will sing praise to my God as long as I live. May my meditation be pleasing to him, as I rejoice in the LORD.

PSALM 104:33-34

*L*ORD, I pray not for tranquility, nor that my tribulations may cease; I pray for your spirit and your love, that you grant me strength and grace to overcome adversity; through Jesus Christ. Amen.

GIROLAMO SAVONAROLA (adapted)

God likes to see his people shut up to this, that there is no hope but in prayer. Herein lies the church's power against the world.   ANDREW BONAR

Give thanks to the Lord, call on his name; make known among the nations what he has done. Sing to him, sing praise to him; tell of all his wonderful acts.
PSALM 105:1-2

I A PILGRIM of eternity, stand before Thee, O eternal One. Let me not seek to deaden or destroy the desire for Thee that disturbs my heart. Let me rather yield myself to its constraint and go where it leads me. Make me wise to see all things today under the form of eternity, and make me brave to face all the changes in my life which such a vision may entail: through the grace of Christ my Saviour. Amen.
JOHN BAILLIE

Look, as a painted man is no man, and as painted fire is no fire, so a cold prayer is no prayer.
THOMAS BROOKS

He sent a man before them—Joseph, sold as a slave.
They bruised his feet with shackles, his neck was
put in irons, till what he foretold came to pass, till
the word of the LORD proved him true.

PSALM 105:17-19

I BESEECH Thee, my most gracious God, preserve me from the cares of this life, lest I should be too much entangled therein; also from the many necessities of the body, lest I should be ensnared by pleasure; and from whatsoever is an obstacle to the soul, lest, being broken with troubles, I should be overthrown. Give me the strength to resist, patience to endure, and constancy to persevere. Amen.

THOMAS À KEMPIS

Are we weak and heavy laden,
Cumbered with a load of care?
Precious Saviour, still our refuge,
Take it to the Lord in prayer.   JOSEPH SCRIVEN

[The Israelites] *asked, and* [*the* LORD] *brought them quail and satisfied them with the bread of heaven. He opened the rock, and water gushed out; like a river it flowed in the desert.*

PSALM 105:40-41

FATHER, I have much to be grateful for tonight, and I thank you. I have much to regret and I ask your forgiveness. But even as I ask your forgiveness I know that I receive it, and a deep peace fills my heart.

Help me to sleep well tonight and to wake ready for that daily yet greatest of gifts, a fresh start.   AVERY BROOKE

Though we cannot by our prayers give God any information, yet we must by our prayers give him honor.   MATTHEW HENRY

Who can proclaim the mighty acts of the LORD *or fully declare his praise? Blessed are they who maintain justice, who constantly do what is right.*

PSALM 106:2-3

SINCE it is of your mercy, O gracious Father, that another day is added to my life; I here dedicate both my soul and my body to you and your service, in a sober, righteous, and godly life: in which resolution do you, O merciful God, confirm and strengthen me; that, as I grow in age, I may grow in grace, and in the knowledge of my Lord and Savior Jesus Christ. Amen.

THE BOOK OF COMMON PRAYER (adapted)

Prayer at its best is the expression of the total life, for all things else being equal, our prayers are only as powerful as our lives.   A. W. TOZER

*[The Israelites] forgot the God who saved them,
who had done great things in Egypt. . . . So he said
he would destroy them.*   PSALM 106:21, 23

O GOD, you are the light of the world, the
desire of all nations, and the shepherd
of our souls: let your light shine in the
darkness, that all the ends of the earth may see
the salvation of our God. By the lifting up of your
Cross gather the peoples to your obedience; let
your sheep hear your voice and be brought
home to your fold so that there may be one flock,
one shepherd, one holy kingdom of righteousness
and peace, one God and Father of all, above all,
and in all, and through all.   W. E. ORCHARD

In Fellowship; alone
   To God with Faith draw near,
Approach His Courts, besiege His Throne
   With all the power of Prayer.

                              CHARLES WESLEY

Praise be to the LORD, the God of Israel, from everlasting to everlasting. Let all the people say, "Amen." Praise the LORD.   PSALM 106:48

O MY GOD! Your fullness of love and of glory is like a boundless ocean—infinite and inconceivable. I bless You that, in revealing Your Son, it pleased You that all the fullness of the Godhead should dwell in Him bodily, that in Him we might see that fullness in human life and weakness. I bless You that His Church on earth is even now, in all its weakness, His body, the fullness of Him that fills all in all; that in Him we are made full; that by the mighty working of Your Spirit, and the indwelling of Your Son, and the knowledge of Your love, we may be filled to all the fullness of God.

ANDREW MURRAY

God may turn his ears from prattling prayers, or preaching prayers, but never from penitent, believing prayers.   WILLIAM S. PLUMER

Give thanks to the LORD, for he is good; his love endures forever.   PSALM 107:1

O GREAT COMPANION of my soul, do go with me today and comfort me by the sense of Your presence in the hours of spiritual isolation. Give me a single eye for duty. Guide me by the voice within. May I take heed of all the judgments of men and gather patiently whatever truth they hold, but teach me still to test them by the words and the spirit of the One who alone is my Master. Amen.

WALTER RAUSCHENBUSCH (adapted)

Most Christians expect little from God, ask little, and therefore receive little and are content with little.   A. W. PINK

I will praise you, O LORD, among the nations; I will sing of you among the peoples. For great is your love, higher than the heavens; your faithfulness reaches to the skies.   PSALM 108:3-4

*L*ORD JESUS, you are all I want and I find in you more than I could possibly need. Lord, though I know this now and swear that I will never leave you, yet I realize I will go searching after other things in order to fulfill my never-ending wants and desires. Fountain of everlasting life, spring up in my heart and satisfy all my needs so that I will never wish to leave you again.

MICHAEL HOLLINGS and ETTA GULLICK

Sincerity is the prime requisite in every approach to the God who requires "Truth in the inward parts" and who hates all hypocrisy, falsehood, and deceit.

GEOFFREY B. WILSON

With my mouth I will greatly extol the LORD; *in the great throng I will praise him. For he stands at the right hand of the needy one, to save his life from those who condemn him.*   PSALM 109:30-31

O THOU eternal God, who hast promised that the kingdoms of this world shall become the Kingdom of our Lord and Saviour Jesus Christ, increase our faith. We believe, but help our unbelief. Thou dost speak to us with the still small voice, but speak also with the voices of the years. Help us to see Thee walking triumphantly across the pages of the past. And hasten the time, we pray, when swords shall be beaten into plowshares, when every knee shall bow and every tongue confess Thee Lord. Amen.   RALPH S. CUSHMAN

If we be empty and poor, it is not because God's hand is straitened, but ours is not opened.

THOMAS MANTON

*The Lord is at your right hand; he will crush kings
on the day of his wrath.*   PSALM 110:5

HEAVENLY FATHER, in your word you
have given us a vision of that holy city
to which the nations of the world bring
their glory: Behold and visit, we pray, the cities
of the earth. Renew the ties of mutual regard
which form our civic life. Send us honest and
able leaders. Enable us to eliminate poverty, pre-
judice, and oppression, that peace may prevail
with righteousness, and justice with order, and
that men and women from different cultures and
with differing talents may find with one another
the fulfillment of their humanity; through Jesus
Christ our Lord. Amen

THE BOOK OF COMMON PRAYER

Prayer is the sovereign remedy.   ROBERT HALL

*The fear of the LORD is the beginning of wisdom; all
who follow his precepts have good understanding.
To him belongs eternal praise.*   PSALM 111:10

FATHER, the very last thing that happened
to me yesterday was that I got offended.
Today that offense is still painfully present
in my heart. I am afraid of it and of what it may
cause me to say to the one I love. I know that you
forgive me in the same way that I forgive others.
So, oh please, flood me with forgiveness! I want
to put away all bitterness and wrath and anger
and wrangling. I open to you, dear God! Today,
in this, I pray that I could be kind, tenderhearted,
and loving; forgiving just as you in Christ have
forgiven me.

By faith in your word and in your Son, I thank
you.   DANIEL PARTNER

*No prayers can be heard which do not come from a
forgiving heart.*   J. C. RYLE

*Praise the LORD. Blessed is the man who fears the
LORD, who finds great delight in his commands.*

PSALM 112:1

GRANT unto me your servant:
    To my God—a heart of flame
    To my fellow men—a heart of love
To myself—a heart of steel.

AUGUSTINE (adapted)

*There is no effort comparable with prayer to God.
When you undertake any other good work, and
persevere in it, you gain rest. But prayer is a battle
all the way to the last breath.*

THE DESERT FATHERS

Let the name of the LORD be praised, both now and forevermore. From the rising of the sun to the place where it sets, the name of the LORD is to be praised.

PSALM 113:2-3

I RESIGN into your hands my sleeping body, my cold hearth and open door. Give me to awaken with smiles; give me to labor smiling. As the sun returns in the east, so let my patience be renewed with dawn; as the sun lightens the world, so let my loving-kindness make bright this house of my habitation.

ROBERT LOUIS STEVENSON (adapted)

We lie to God in prayer if we do not rely on him afterwards.   ROBERT LEIGHTON

Not to us, O LORD, not to us but to your name be the glory, because of your love and faithfulness.

PSALM 115:1

I GIVE you thanks, O God, for those who mean so much to me—
Those to whom I can go at any time.
Those with whom I can talk and keep nothing back, knowing that they will not laugh at my dreams or my failures.
Those in whose presence it is easier to be good.
Those who by their warning have held me back from mistakes I might have made.
Above all, I thank you for Jesus Christ, Lord of my heart and Savior of my soul, in whose Name I offer this thanksgiving.

WILLIAM BARCLAY (adapted)

You have given so much to me,
Give one thing more, a grateful heart.

GEORGE HERBERT

I love the LORD, for he heard my voice; he heard my cry for mercy. Because he turned his ear to me, I will call on him as long as I live.   PSALM 116:1-2

SINCE your departure from Olivet's
        Mountain,
        Why is your coming again so delayed?
Thru the long years we have longed for your
        coming
    Have you not heard all the prayers that we've
        prayed?

Beloved Lord, since the year you ascended
    Everything here has been tasteless and dry;
Often in praying and often in watching,
    In every movement, for you, Lord, we sigh.

O Lord, remember the days have been lengthened
    Since you have promised ere going away;
We hope and hope and are endlessly hoping,
    That you will come. Can you come e'en today?
                                    WATCHMAN NEE

*Prayer is the heavenly telephone that brings
    The distant near, till heaven to earth
        comes down.*   A. B. SIMPSON

Praise the LORD, all you nations; extol him, all you peoples. For great is his love toward us, and the faithfulness of the LORD endures forever. Praise the LORD.   PSALM 117:1-2

ALMIGHTY GOD, who sent the Spirit of truth to me to guide me into all truth: so rule my life by your power that I may be truthful in thought and word and deed. May no fear or hope ever make me false in act or speech; cast out from me whatsoever loves or makes a lie, and bring me into the perfect freedom of your truth, through Jesus Christ our Lord.

BROOKE FOSS WESTCOTT (adapted)

The granting of prayer, when offered in the name of Jesus, reveals the Father's love to him, and the honor which he has put upon him.

CHARLES H. SPURGEON

I was pushed back and about to fall, but the LORD helped me. The LORD is my strength and my song; he has become my salvation.   PSALM 118:13-14

*O*LORD, prepare my heart, I beseech you, to reverence you, to adore you, to love you; to hate, for love of you, all my sins and imperfections, short-comings, whatever in me displeases you; and to love all which you love. Give me, Lord, fervor of love, shame for my unthankfulness, sorrow for my sins, longing for your grace, and to be wholly united with you. Let my very coldness call for the glow of your love; let my emptiness and dryness, like a barren and thirsty land, thirst for you, call on you to come into my soul, who refreshes those who are weary. Let my heart ache to you and for you, who stills the aching of the heart. Let my mute longings praise you, crave you, who satisfies the empty soul that waits on you.

E. B. PUSEY

Nothing is discussed more and practiced less than prayer.   ANONYMOUS

The stone the builders rejected has become the capstone; the LORD has done this, and it is marvelous in our eyes. This is the day the LORD has made; let us rejoice and be glad in it.

PSALM 118:22-24

*L*ORD JESUS, I confess I am not able to comprehend what it meant for you to lay aside your glory and condescend to spend thirty-three years here on earth, a period of hardship, rejection, malice, and finally the most agonizing form of death.
Your incarnation means uttermost love for
        unlovely sinners like me.
It means pardon for me.
It means peace for me.
It means hope of glory.
It is the most wonderful message the
        world has ever heard and I am a
        beneficiary of what you did!
Amen! Hallelujah!   ROBERT C. SAVAGE

Straight praying is never born of crooked conduct.

E. M. BOUNDS

I seek you with all my heart; do not let me stray from your commands. I have hidden your word in my heart that I might not sin against you.

PSALM 119:10-11

GIVE ME, O Lord
        unlimited patience
        unlimited understanding
    unlimited love
Then I will be able to forgive
    as I have been forgiven
to bless
    as I have been blessed. Amen.   DENIS DUNCAN

The great thing in prayer is to feel that we are putting our supplications into the bosom of omnipotent love.   ANDREW MURRAY

I hold fast to your statutes, O LORD; do not let me be put to shame. I run in the path of your commands, for you have set my heart free.

PSALM 119:31-32

ALMIGHTY GOD, Father of all mercies, we your unworthy servants give you most humble and hearty thanks for all your goodness and loving-kindness to us, and to all. We bless you for your creation, preservation, and all the blessings of this life; but above all, for your inestimable love in the redemption of the world by our Lord Jesus Christ; for the means of grace, and for the hope of glory. And, we beg you, give us that due sense of all your mercies, that our hearts may be unfeignedly thankful, and that we show forth your praise, not only with our lips, but in our lives: by giving up ourselves to your service and by walking before you in holiness and righteousness all our days; through Jesus Christ our Lord, to whom with you and the Holy Spirit be all honor and glory, world without end.

THE BOOK OF COMMON PRAYER

Thanks be unto God for his unspeakable gift.

2 CORINTHIANS 9:15, *KJV*

Turn my heart toward your statutes and not toward selfish gain. Turn my eyes away from worthless things; preserve my life according to your word.

PSALM 119:36-37

ALMIGHTY and Holy Spirit, the Comforter, pure, living, true—illumine, govern, sanctify me, and confirm my heart and mind in the faith, and in all genuine consolation; preserve and rule over me so that, dwelling in the house of the Lord, all the days of my life, I may behold the Lord and praise him with a joyful spirit, and in union with all the heavenly church. Amen.   PHILIP MELANCHTHON

No heart thrives without much secret converse with God and nothing will make amends for the want of it.

JOHN BERRIDGE

In the night I remember your name, O LORD, and I will keep your law. This has been my practice: I obey your precepts.   PSALM 119:55-56

O GOD of peace, entirely sanctify me; keep my spirit and soul and body sound and blameless at the coming of our Lord Jesus Christ. You are the one who calls me, you are faithful, and you will do this.

1 THESSALONIANS 5:23-24 (adapted)

We read of preaching the Word out of season, but we do not read of praying out of season, for that is never out of season.   MATTHEW HENRY

May your unfailing love be my comfort, according to your promise to your servant. Let your compassion come to me that I may live, for your law is my delight.   PSALM 119:76-77

O THOU who camest from above,
The pure celestial fire to impart,
Kindle a flame of sacred love
On the mean altar of my heart.

There let it for thy glory burn
With inextinguishable blaze,
And trembling to its source return
In humble prayer, and fervent praise.

CHARLES WESLEY

The spirit of prayer is the fruit and token of the Spirit of adoption.   JOHN NEWTON

Your word, O LORD, is eternal; it stands firm in the heavens. Your faithfulness continues through all generations; you established the earth, and it endures.   PSALM 119:89-90

M Y FATHER, do with me as you will, only help me against myself and for you; I am your child, the inheritor of your spirit, your being, a part of yourself, glorious in you, but grown poor in me: let me be your dog, your horse, your anything, anything you will; let me be yours in any shape the love that is my Father may please to have me; let me be yours in any way, and my own or another's in no way but yours.   GEORGE MACDONALD

Prayers are the leeches of care.   ANONYMOUS

Your word is a lamp to my feet and a light for my path. I have taken an oath and confirmed it, that I will follow your righteous laws.

PSALM 119:105-106

YOUR words were found, and I ate them, and your words became to me a joy and the delight of my heart;
for I am called by your name,
O LORD, God of hosts.   JEREMIAH 15:16, NRSV

The mightier any is in the Word, the more mighty he will be in prayer.   WILLIAM GURNALL

I hate double-minded men, but I love your law. You are my refuge and my shield; I have put my hope in your word.   PSALM 119:113-114

O JESUS
Be the canoe that holds me in the
sea of life.
Be the steer that keeps me straight.
Be the outrigger that supports me in times
of great temptation.
Let thy Spirit be my sail that carries me
through each day.
Keep my body strong,
so that I can paddle steadfastly on,
in the long voyage of life.

A NEW HEBRIDEAN PRAYER

Prayer is not conquering God's reluctance, but taking hold of God's willingness. PHILLIPS BROOKS

Righteous are you, O LORD, and your laws are right. The statutes you have laid down are righteous; they are fully trustworthy.

PSALM 119:137-138

GRANT to me, O Lord, to know what I ought to know, to love what I ought to love, to praise what delights you most, to value what is precious in your sight, to hate what is offensive to you. Do not suffer me to judge according to the sight of my eyes, nor to pass sentence according to the hearing of the ears of ignorant men; but to discern with true judgment between things visible and spiritual, and above all things to enquire what is the good pleasure of your will.   THOMAS À KEMPIS

Prayer is and remains always a native and deepest impulse of the soul of man.   THOMAS CARLYLE

I long for your salvation, O LORD, and your law is my delight. Let me live that I may praise you, and may your laws sustain me.   PSALM 119:174-175

FROM the cowardice that dare not face
      new truth
      From the laziness that is contented with
         half truth
From the arrogance that thinks it knows
      all truth,
Good Lord, deliver me.   A PRAYER FROM KENYA

Two went to pray? Oh, rather say
One went to brag, the other to pray;
One stands up close and treads on high
Where the other dares not send his eye;
One nearer to God's altar trod,
the other to the altar's God.

RICHARD CRANSHAW, *Luke 18:9-14*

I call on the LORD in my distress, and he answers me. Save me, O LORD, from lying lips and from deceitful tongues.   PSALM 120:1-2

GRANT, O God, that we may wait patiently, as servants standing before their Lord, to know your will; that we may welcome all truth, under whatever outward form it may be uttered; that we may bless every good deed, by whomsoever it may be done; that we may rise above all strife to the contemplation of your eternal truth and goodness; through Jesus Christ our Savior.   CHARLES KINGSLEY

Faith is the fountain of prayer, and prayer should be nothing else but faith exercised.

                    THOMAS MANTON

The LORD will keep you from all harm—he will watch over your life; the LORD will watch over your coming and going both now and forevermore.

PSALM 121:7-8

OUR FATHER in heaven, I thank you that you have led me into the light. I thank you for sending the Savior to call me from death to life. I confess that I was dead in sin before I heard his call, but when I heard him, like Lazarus, I arose. But, O my Father, the grave clothes bind me still. Old habits that I cannot throw off, old customs that are so much a part of my life that I am helpless to live the new life that Christ calls me to live. Give me strength, O Father, to break the bonds; give me courage to live a new life in you, give me faith, to believe that with your help I cannot fail. And this I ask in the Savior's name who has taught me to come to you.   A PRAYER FROM TAIWAN

No time is so well spent in every day as that which we spend upon our knees.   J. C. RYLE

I rejoiced with those who said to me, "Let us go to the house of the LORD." Our feet are standing in your gates, O Jerusalem.   PSALM 122:1-2

GIVE ME
        The girdle, the helmet,
        The breastplate, the shield,
The shoes, the sword,
        over all, prayer.
Grant me the power and the opportunity of
            welldoing
    that before the day of my decease
    I may at all adventure effect some good thing
        whereof the fruit may remain:
that I may be able to appear with righteousness
        and be satisfied with glory.
And grant me a good end—
    What is above every gift—a good a holy end
        of life,
    a glorious and joyful resurrection.
                        LANCELOT ANDREWES (adapted)

Amazing things start happening when we start praying!   ANONYMOUS

As the eyes of slaves look to the hand of their master, as the eyes of a maid look to the hand of her mistress, so our eyes look to the LORD our God, till he shows us his mercy.   PSALM 123:2

*L*ET NO riches make me ever forget myself, no poverty make me to forget you: let no hope or fear, no pleasure or pain, no accident without, no weakness within, hinder or discompose my duty, or turn me from the ways of your commandments. O let your Spirit dwell with me forever, and make my soul just and charitable, full of honesty, full of religion, resolute and constant in holy purposes, but inflexible to evil. Make me humble and obedient, peaceable and pious: let me never envy any man's good, nor deserve to be despised myself: and if I be, teach me to bear it with meekness and charity.   JEREMY TAYLOR

Sometimes we think we are too busy to pray. That is a great mistake, for praying is a saving of time.
                    CHARLES H. SPURGEON

We have escaped like a bird out of the fowler's snare; the snare has been broken, and we have escaped. Our help is in the name of the LORD, the Maker of heaven and earth.   PSALM 124:7-8

HELP each one of us, gracious Father, to live in such magnanimity and restraint that the Head of the church may never have cause to say to any one of us, This is my body, broken by you.   A PRAYER FROM CHINA

Every time you pray, if your prayer is sincere, there will be new feeling and new meaning in it which will give you fresh courage, and you will understand that prayer is an education.

FEODOR DOSTOEVSKI, *The Brothers Karamozov*

Those who trust in the LORD *are like Mount Zion,*
which cannot be shaken but endures forever.

PSALM 125:1

O GOD, Make the door of this house wide
enough to receive all who need human
love and fellowship, and a heavenly
Father's care; and narrow enough to shut out all
envy, pride and hate.

Make its threshold smooth enough to be no
stumbling-block to children, nor to straying feet,
but rugged enough to turn back the tempter's
power:

Make it a gateway to thine eternal kingdom.

THOMAS KEN

Those who always pray are necessary to those who
never pray.   VICTOR HUGO

When the LORD brought back the captives to Zion,
we were like men who dreamed. Our mouths were
filled with laughter, our tongues with songs of joy.
Then it was said among the nations, "The LORD has
done great things for them."   PSALM 126:1-2

INSPIRE rulers and peoples with counsels of meekness. Heal the discords that tear nations asunder. You who did shed your precious blood that they might live as brothers, bring men together once more in loving harmony. To the cry of the Apostle Peter: "Save us, Lord, we perish," you did answer words of mercy and did still the raging waves. Stoop now to hear our trustful prayers and give back to the world order and peace.   POPE BENEDICT XV

The spectacle of a nation praying is more
awe-inspiring than the explosion of an atomic
bomb. The force of prayer is greater than any
possible combination of man-controlled power,
because prayer is man's greatest means of trapping
the infinite resources of God.   J. EDGAR HOOVER

Sons are a heritage from the LORD, children a reward from him. Like arrows in the hands of a warrior are sons born in one's youth. Blessed is the man whose quiver is full of them.   PSALM 127:3-5

FATHER, I really thank you for my family. Sometimes I take them for granted, in the hustle and bustle and challenges of my daily life. Help me to take a long look at them today, and see what I can do—with your help—to demonstrate my love. In Jesus' name.

PAT BOONE

I know not by what methods rare,
   But this I know: God answers prayer.
I know not if the blessing sought
   Will come in just the guise I thought.
I leave my prayer to Him alone
   Whose will is wiser than my own.

ELIZA M. HICKOK

Blessed are all who fear the LORD, who walk in his
ways. You will eat the fruit of your labor; blessings
and prosperity will be yours.   PSALM 128:1-2

O GOD, I thank you because, when I have
been for some time interrupted in my
work and my thoughts of you have
been diverted, I have found how pleasing it is to
my mind to feel the motions of your Spirit
quickening me and exciting me to return.

SUSANNA WESLEY

To God your every Want
    In instant Prayer display,
Pray always; pray, and never faint;
    Pray, without ceasing Pray.   CHARLES WESLEY

Plowmen have plowed my back and made their furrows long. But the LORD is righteous; he has cut me free from the cords of the wicked.

PSALM 129:3-4

*B*LESSED LORD, who was tempted in all things like as we are, have mercy upon my frailty. Out of weakness give me strength. Grant to me your fear that I may fear only you. Support me in time of temptation. Embolden me in the time of danger. Help me to do your work with good courage, and to continue your faithful soldier and servant unto my life's end; through Jesus Christ our Lord.

BROOKE FOSS WESTCOTT (adapted)

Prayers are heard in heaven very much in proportion to your faith. Little faith will get very great mercies, but great faith still greater.

CHARLES H. SPURGEON

Out of the depths I cry to you, O LORD; O Lord, hear my voice. Let your ears be attentive to my cry for mercy.   PSALM 130:1-2

*O*LORD, when I am bewildered and the world is all noise and confusion around me and I don't know which way to go and am frightened, then be with me. Put your hand on my shoulder and let your strength invade my weakness and your light burn the mist from my mind. Help me to step forward with faith in the way I should go.

AVERY BROOKE

We, on our side, are praying to Him to give us victory, because we believe we are right; but those on the other side pray to Him, too, for victory, believing they are right. What must He think of us?

ABRAHAM LINCOLN

My heart is not proud, O LORD, my eyes are not haughty. . . . But I have stilled and quieted my soul; like a weaned child with its mother.

PSALM 131:1-2

DON'T MAKE me good, Lord.
        Make me yours.
    If all I am is good
And I give it,
    Then I give myself only.
But if I'm yours
    when I give myself,
        I give you.
And those I love
    don't need me, good or bad.
        They need you.
So, make me yours.   JOHN B. COBURN

Don't be timid when you pray; rather, batter the very gates of heaven with storms of prayer.

ANONYMOUS

Let us go to his dwelling place; let us worship at his footstool—arise, O LORD, and come to your resting place, you and the ark of your might.

PSALM 132:7-8

H oly Spirit, truth divine,
Dawn upon this soul of mine;
Word of God and inward light,
Wake my spirit, clear my sight.

Holy Spirit, love divine,
Glow within this heart of mine,
Kindle every high desire,
Purge me now in thy pure fire.

Holy Spirit, peace divine,
Still this restless heart of mine,
Speak to calm this tossing sea,
Stayed in thy tranquility.

Holy Spirit, joy divine,
Gladden thou this heart of mine;
In the desert ways I'll sing,
Spring, O well, forever spring.

SAMUEL LONGFELLOW

It is not well for man to pray cream, and live skim milk.   HENRY WARD BEECHER

How good and pleasant it is when brothers live together in unity! It is like precious oil poured on the head, running down on the beard.

PSALM 133:1-2

ALMIGHTY GOD, our heavenly Father, who sets the solitary in families; we commend to your continual care the homes in which your people dwell. Put far from them, we beseech you, every root of bitterness, the desire of vain-glory, and the pride of life. Fill them with faith, virtue, knowledge, temperance, patience, godliness. Knit together in constant affection those who, in holy wedlock, have been made one flesh; turn the heart of the fathers to the children, and the heart to the children to the fathers; and so enkindle fervent charity among us all, that we be evermore kindly affectioned with brotherly love; through Jesus Christ our Lord. Amen.   *THE BOOK OF COMMON PRAYER*

For You, O LORD of hosts, God of Israel, have revealed this to Your servant, saying, "I will build you a house." Therefore Your servant found it in his heart to pray this prayer to You.

2 SAMUEL 7:27, NKJV

Lift up your hands in the sanctuary and praise the LORD. May the LORD, the Maker of heaven and earth, bless you from Zion.   PSALM 134:2-3

GRANT, Almighty God, that as you shine on me by your Word, I may not be blind at midday, nor willfully seek darkness, and thus lull my mind asleep: but, may I be roused daily by your words, and may I stir up myself more and more to fear your name and thus present myself and all my pursuits, as a sacrifice to you, that you may peaceably rule and perpetually dwell in me, until you gather me to your celestial habitation, where there is reserved for me eternal rest and glory, through Jesus Christ our Lord. Amen.   JOHN CALVIN (adapted)

Prayer is a strong wall and fortress of the church: it is a goodly Christian weapon.   MARTIN LUTHER

I know that the Lord is great, that our Lord is greater than all gods. The Lord does whatever pleases him, in the heavens and on the earth, in the seas and all their depths.   PSALM 135:5-6

O GOD, light of the minds that see you, life of the souls that love you, and strength of the souls that seek you, enlarge my mind and raise the vision of my heart, that, with swift wings of thought, my spirit may reach you, the eternal wisdom, you who live from everlasting to everlasting; through Jesus Christ our Lord. Amen.

AUGUSTINE (adapted)

The man who prays grows, and the muscles of the soul swell from this whipcord to iron bands.

F. B. MEYER

Give thanks to the LORD, for he is good. His love
endures forever.   PSALM 136:1

I LOVE YOU, O my God; and I desire to love
you more and more. Grant to me that I may
love you as much as I desire, and as much
as I ought. O dearest Friend, who has so loved
and saved me, the thought of whom is so sweet
and always growing sweeter, watch over my lips,
my steps, my deeds, and I shall not need to be
anxious either for my soul or my body. Give me
love, sweetest of all gifts, which knows no
enemy. Give me in my heart pure love, born of
your love to me, that I may love others as you
love me. O most loving Father of Jesus Christ,
from whom flows all love, let my heart, frozen in
sin, cold to you and cold to others, be warmed
by this divine fire. So help and bless me in your
Son. Amen.   ANSELM OF CANTERBURY (adapted)

Prayer is not eloquence, but earnestness; not the
definition of helplessness, but the feeling of it; not
figures of speech, but earnestness of soul.

HANNAH MORE

*By the rivers of Babylon we sat down and wept
when we remembered Zion . . . for there our captors
asked us for songs, our tormentors demanded songs
of joy.* PSALM 137:1, 3

O GOD, you gave us the grace to carry the sword of your kingdom of peace; and you made us messengers of peace in a world of strife, and messengers of strife in a world of false peace: make strong our hand, make clear our voice, give us humility with firmness and insight with passion, that we may fight, not to conquer, but to redeem.

GREGORY VLASTOS

*Prayer is not artful monologue
   Of voice uplifted from the son;
It is Love's tender dialogue
   Between the soul and God.*

JOHN RICHARD MORELAND

I will praise you, O LORD, with all my heart; before the "gods" I will sing your praise. I will bow down toward your holy temple and will praise your name for your love and your faithfulness.

PSALM 138:1-2

O LORD CHRIST, who, when your hour was come, went without fear amongst those who sought your life: grant us grace to confess you before all, without arrogance and without fear, that your Holy Name may be glorified.   J. H. OLDHAM

Prayer is not merely an occasional impulse to which we respond when we are in trouble: prayer is a life attitude.   WALTER A. MUELLER

Where can I go from your Spirit? Where can I flee from your presence? If I go up to the heavens, you are there; if I make my bed in the depths, you are there.   PSALM 139:7-8

THOUGH it has not happened to me, I know and love some to whom it has happened, Lord. They are yours and they are my fellows, but they have drifted on to drugs. There are so may reasons, Lord. You know them, I can only try to sense them. They are shy, they are weak, they can't communicate, they're misfits, their homes don't work, they want to belong, they want to be loved, Lord. Give them your understanding when we don't understand them; give them your strength when they feel the craving; above all, let them feel your love in you and through us. Help them, Lord.

MICHAEL HOLLINGS and ETTA GULLICK

The effectual fervent prayer of a righteous man availeth much.   JAMES 5:16, *KJV*

I know that the LORD secures justice for the poor and upholds the cause of the needy. Surely the righteous will praise your name and the upright will live before you. PSALM 140:12-13

WHEN days are cold and grey and
          short,
        and nights grow long,
Cause me God to sing this song:
    The Word became flesh.

When friends and loves and lives can't know
    my pain, my fear,
Open up my ears to hear:
    The Word became flesh.

When heart and will and thought presume
    you're far away,
Let me touch the truth and say:
    The Word became flesh.

Since Word and flesh and life were one
    to show your love,
Lift human eyes to see above:
    The Word became flesh.   DANIEL PARTNER

Constant prayer quickly straightens out our thoughts.   THE DESERT FATHERS

But my eyes are fixed on you, O Sovereign LORD; in you I take refuge—do not give me over to death.

PSALM 141:8

O UT of my bondage, sorrow, and night,
      Jesus, I come! Jesus I come!
      Into Thy freedom, gladness, and light,
Jesus, I come to Thee!
Out of my sickness into Thy health,
Out of my want and into Thy wealth,
Out of my sin and into Thyself,
    Jesus, I come to Thee!

Out of my shameful failure and loss,
    Jesus, I come! Jesus I come!
Into the glorious gain of Thy cross,
    Jesus, I come to Thee!
Out of earth's sorrows into Thy balm,
Out of life's storm and into Thy calm,
Out of distress to jubilant psalm,
    Jesus, I come to Thee!   WILLIAM T. SLEEPER

My house shall be called the house of prayer.

MATTHEW 21:13, *KJV*

Set me free from my prison, that I may praise your name. Then the righteous will gather about me because of your goodness to me.   PSALM 142:7

O CHRIST, you were called the man of sorrows, and yet you prayed for your disciples that they might have your joy; grant me such sympathy as takes upon itself the burden for the sorrowing; and with it such glad courage as shall turn the way of sadness into the way of joy, because we follow in your footsteps, O blessed Master, Jesus Christ. Amen.

WALTER RUSSELL BOWIE (adapted)

Prayer crowns God with the honor and glory due to His name, and God crowns prayer with assurance and comfort. The most praying souls are the most assured souls.   THOMAS BROOKS

Let the morning bring me word of your unfailing love, for I have put my trust in you. Show me the way I should go, for to you I lift up my soul.

PSALM 143:8

O HOLY CHILD of Bethlehem,
Descend on us, we pray;
Cast out our sin, and enter in,
Be born in us today.
We hear the Christmas angels
The great glad tidings tell;
O come to us, abide in us,
Our Lord Emmanuel! Amen.   PHILLIPS BROOKS

Jesus Christ is a God whom we approach without pride, and before whom we humble ourselves without despair.   BLAISE PASCAL

*O LORD, what is man that you care for him, the son
of man that you think of him?*   PSALM 144:3

WE YEARN, our Father, for the simple beauty of Christmas—for all the
old familiar melodies and words
that remind us of that great miracle when He
who had made all things was one night to come
as a babe, to lie in the crook of a woman's arm.

Before such mystery we kneel, as we follow
the shepherds and Wise Men to bring Thee the
gift of our love—a love we confess has not
always been as warm or sincere or real as it
should have been. But now, on this Christmas
Day, that love would find its Beloved, and from
Thee receive the grace to make it pure again,
warm and real.

May the loving-kindness of Christmas not
only creep into our hearts, but there abide, so
that not even the return to earthly cares and
responsibilities, not all the festivities of our own
devising may cause it to creep away weeping.
May the joy and spirit of Christmas stay with us
now and forever.   PETER MARSHALL

The simple heart that freely asks in love, obtains.
                        JOHN GREENLEAF WHITTIER

The LORD is gracious and compassionate, slow to anger and rich in love. The LORD is good to all; he has compassion on all he has made.

PSALM 145:8-9

WHAT MIRACLES of the human
spirit are Yours, O God.
There is so much that seems so
often without hope to us;
so much that hangs heavy on our minds;
so much that is a burden and a heartache
to us, Lord.
And then You come on wings of love and say:
"Let not your heart be troubled . . . peace
be unto you.
In the world ye shall have tribulation, but
be of good cheer,
I have overcome the world!"
O Jesus Christ, You are indeed the light of the
world, and in You is no darkness at
all!

ARTHUR A. ROUNER, JR.

Always look for ways to act upon the faith you display in your prayers.   ANONYMOUS

Blessed is he whose help is the God of Jacob, whose hope is in the LORD his God, the Maker of heaven and earth, the sea, and everything in them—the LORD, who remains faithful forever.   PSALM 146:5-6

I ACKNOWLEDGED my sin to you,
   and I did not hide my iniquity;
   I said, "I will confess my transgressions to
     the LORD."
 and you forgave the guilt of my sin.

Therefore let all who are faithful
   offer prayer to you;
at a time of distress, the rush of mighty waters
   shall not reach them.
You are a hiding place for me;
   you preserve me from trouble;
   you surround me with glad cries of
              deliverance.   PSALM 32:5-7, *NRSV*

We must pray for more prayer, for it is the world's mightiest healing force.   FRANK C. LAUBACH

Sing to the LORD with thanksgiving; make music to our God on the harp. He covers the sky with clouds; he supplies the earth with rain and makes grass grow on the hills.   PSALM 147:7-8

*L*ET me not seek outside of you what I can
      only find in you, O Lord.
     Peace and rest, and joy and bliss,
  which abide only in your abiding joy.
Lift up my soul above the weary round
        of harassing thoughts to your
        eternal presence.
Lift up my mind to the pure, bright, serene
        atmosphere of your presence,
    that I may breathe freely,
    there repose in your love,
    there be at rest from myself
    and from all things that weary me:
and thence return, arrayed in your peace,
      to do and to bear
  whatsoever shall best please you, O blessed
      Lord.   E. B. PUSEY

Watch and pray, lest you enter into temptation.
                   MATTHEW 26:41, *NKJV*

*Praise him, you highest heavens and you waters
above the skies. Let them praise the name of the
Lord, for he commanded and they were created.*

PSALM 148:4-5

O GOD of steadfastness and encourage-
ment, grant all Christians to live in
harmony with one another in accordance with Christ Jesus, so that together we may
with one voice glorify the God and Father of our
Lord Jesus Christ.

You are the God of hope. May you fill us with
all joy and peace in believing, so that we may
abound in hope by the power of the Holy Spirit.

O God of all peace, be with all of us. Amen.

ROMANS 15:5-6, 13, 33 (adapted)

*Though I am weak, yet God, when prayed,
Cannot withhold his conquering aid.*

RALPH WALDO EMERSON

Praise the LORD. Sing to the LORD a new song, his praise in the assembly of the saints.

PSALM 149:1

BREAK Thou the Bread of Life,
    Dear Lord, to me,
    As Thou didst break the loaves
  Beside the sea;
Beyond the sacred page
  I seek Thee, Lord;
My spirit pants for Thee,
  O Living Word.

Bless Thou the truth, dear Lord,
  To me, to me,
As Thou didst bless the bread
  By Galilee;
Then shall all bondage cease,
  All fetters fall;
And I shall find my peace,
  My All in all.   MARY A. LATHBURY

Non-praying is lawlessness, discord, anarchy.

E. M. BOUNDS

Praise him with the clash of cymbals, praise him with resounding cymbals. Let everything that has breath praise the LORD. Praise the LORD.

PSALM 150:5-6

AND I offer also for all those whom I have in any way grieved, vexed, oppressed, and scandalized, by word or deed, knowingly or unknowingly; that you may equally forgive us all our sins, and all our offenses against each other.

Take away, O Lord, from our hearts all suspiciousness, indignation, anger, and contention, and whatever is calculated to wound charity, and to lessen brotherly love.

Have mercy, O Lord, have mercy on those who seek your mercy; give grace to the needy; make us so to live, that we may be found worthy to enjoy the fruition of your grace, and that we may attain to eternal life.   THOMAS À KEMPIS

Whenever you stand praying, forgive, if you have anything against anyone; so that your Father in heaven may also forgive you your trespasses.

MARK 11:25, *NRSV*

Author Index

Scripture Index